PRAISE FOR *PEOPLE I MET AT THE GATES OF HEAVEN*

"In this long-awaited book, Don Piper reveals the people who met him at the gates of Heaven after his tragic near-fatal accident in 1989 and how those people helped him get there. He answers compelling questions about what Heaven will be like. But even more importantly he asks the timeless and urgent question: Who's going to be there because of you. It's a book about intentional personal sharing of our faith as we go about our daily lives. It's a clear call to populate Heaven! And do we ever need it now!"

—Michael W. Smith, Multiple Grammy, American Music Award, Dove Award - winning recording artist and composer, Over 18 Million Albums sold

"I've studied over 1000 cases of people who die or are near-death and return, and many speak of a heavenly welcoming committee. In his inspiring new book, Don vividly introduces us to those who welcomed him at the gates of heaven, answering many of our relational questions and motivating us to have a powerful impact on who will be there to welcome us one day."

—John Burke, Senior Pastor, Gateway Church, Austin, Texas, New York Times Best-selling author, *Imagine Heaven*

"A clarion call for every believer who is striving to live with purpose, intentionality, and a conviction for a soulwinning. More than any other generation before us, so many are seeking an answer to the age-old question, "Does my life really matter?" Thankfully, because of Don Piper's courage to share the rest of his story with the world, the answer is crystal clear. No other book provides a more convincing case for genuine evangelism than *People I Met at the Gates of Heaven: Who Is going to Be there because of You?* Readers will be reassured, then inspired to leave a legacy that will live on for eternity."

—Sergio de la Mora, Lead Pastor, Cornerstone Church of San
Diego, Author, Paradox and *The Heart Revolution*

"When I was 15 years old, I met Don Piper and it changed my life, and this was four years before Don went to heaven! Don has touched millions of lives through *90 Minutes in Heaven* and his subsequent books. In *People I Met at the Gates of Heaven*, Don takes you through the journey of his own conversion to Christianity and development of his faith framed by his miraculous visit to heaven. This book not only pays homage to those that so influenced Don in his Christian walk but also emphasizes the urgency for us to share the good news of our Lord and Savior Jesus Christ. A definite must read!"

—T Bradley Edwards, M.D., World-class Orthopedic shoulder
surgeon, Fondren Orthopedic Group, Houston, Texas

"DON'T WAIT. That is what I thought about when I read Don's book. I tragically lost one of my best friends at 27 years old and when asked to eulogize him, I couldn't. I was too emotional and the idea of speaking about eternity at the time was frightening; because, I didn't know where either of us were going to spend eternity. That moment sent me to my knees, where I found the answer was in Jesus Christ. For the last 33 years of my life, I have made every effort to know my friends will meet me at the gate of heaven. Don's perspective is authentic, unique, and truly a treasure. My prayer is that this book will inspire you to make sure that you and your loved ones meet us at the gates of heaven."

—Mark Fincannon, Emmy Award-winning motion picture
Casting Director, Atlanta, Georgia. Mark was Casting Director for
the movie, *90 Minutes in Heaven*.

"In Don Piper's new release, *People I Met At the Gates of Heaven*, Don shares the moving stories of people who met him when he arrived at Heaven's gates, and offers a stirring challenge to the reader to do everything we can during our time here on earth to make sure those close to us, as well as those we encounter only in passing, know of the incredible eternity that they can have in God's Presence. An engaging book that challenges us to personal evangelism, avoiding the "guilt-driven" approach, and instead lovingly encouraging us to make sure everyone we know has an opportunity to join us in Heaven someday."

—Chuck Wallington, President, Christian Supply, Inc.,
Spartanburg, South Carolina, One of the largest Christian
Bookstores in the world

"Don Piper has done it again! Like any fine artist, he has created a masterpiece. In this book, heaven is his canvas. His brush strokes are the stories of those people who influenced his Christian journey and, therefore, paved his way to heaven's gates. These stories are sure to influence our own lives as Don emphasizes the importance that every Christian assist others to get from "here" to "there." Don hands us a paint brush and says, "Start painting." Heaven is waiting for your masterpiece!"

—Harold Hendren, Senior Pastor, New Covenant United Methodist Church, The Villages, Florida

"*People I Met at the Gates of Heaven* gives us an intimate encounter of Don Piper's 90-minute visit there. For the first time, Don reveals who met him at the gates of Heaven and gives us a clear understanding of why they did. These individuals challenge us, as fellow Believers, to understand the serious responsibility we have as Christians. It implores us to contemplate our own eternity and confronts us about *who we will greet* as they enter Eternity. Read this book. It will change the way you love and serve others."

—Diana Wiley, Executive Director & Founder, True Vineyard
Ministries, San Marcos, Texas

"This is the most important, compelling writing I have ever read on the issue of death and dying. Don Piper is God's gift to our generation. He literally died. He was sent back to us with encounters and insights which inspired this great work, I never realized before reading Don's book how important each life is to God's eternal picture. What the world calls death, God calls the beginning. This is a must read. Thank you, Don."

—Stan Cottrell, *Guinness Book of Records* World Distance Runner

"When I read *90 Minutes in Heaven*, my mother had recently passed. This book brought comfort to both me and my father. A short time later, my Dad joined her. As I think of them today, I picture both of their smiling faces. I know WHERE they are and WHO they are with and I WILL see them again.

"I appreciate Don sharing *People I Met at the Gates of Heaven*. While it is personal, it is also both inspirational and confirming. We are saved to serve and tell others about Jesus and how he changed our lives. Half the battle is knowing. The other half is doing.

"There is no guarantee of tomorrow.

"Will we let those we love spend eternity in hell because we don't love them enough to tell them about Jesus? Thank you Don Piper for challenging us to tell our story."

—Paul Robbins, Founder and President, Viking Cold Solutions, Elder,
First Christian Church of the Beaches, Jacksonville Beach, Florida

"In his long-awaited and much anticipated follow-up to his best-selling *90 Minutes in Heaven*, author Don Piper brings readers deep into his personal and deeply touching experience at the gates of Heaven after dying in a car crash. In sharing the intimate details, he gives readers a glorious hope and profound longing for Heaven and gentle conviction to answer the question, "Who will be in Heaven because of you?" His new book, *People I Met at the Gates of Heaven: Who Is Going to Be There Because of You?*, is a *must read* that will convince you that everyone you meet is purposefully and masterfully placed there by God."

—Tonya Frye, *Executive Director*, Get Together Northwest,
Cypress, Texas

BY DON PIPER WITH CECIL MURPHEY

90 Minutes in Heaven: A True Story of Death and Life
by Don Piper with Cecil Murphey

BY DON PIPER AND CECIL MURPHEY

Daily Devotions Inspired by 90 Minutes in Heaven:
90 Readings for Hope and Healing,
by Don Piper and Cecil Murphey

Heaven Is Real: Lessons on Earthly Joy
—from the Man Who Spent 90 Minutes in Heaven
by Don Piper and Cecil Murphey

Getting to Heaven: Departing Instructions for Your Life Now
by Don Piper and Cecil Murphey

People I Met
at the Gates of
HEAVEN

Who Is Going to Be There
Because of You?

DON PIPER
and CECIL MURPHEY

New York Nashville

FaithWords
Hachette Book Group
1290 Avenue of the Americas, New York, NY 10104
faithwords.com
twitter.com/faithwords

Originally published in hardcover and ebook by FaithWords: November 2018

First Trade Paperback Edition: November 2019

FaithWords is a division of Hachette Book Group, Inc. The FaithWords name and logo are trademarks of Hachette Book Group, Inc.

Unless otherwise indicated Scriptures taken from the Holy Bible, New International Version®, NIV®. Copyright © 1973, 1978, 1984, 2011 by Biblica, Inc.™ Used by permission of Zondervan. All rights reserved worldwide. www.zondervan.com The "NIV" and "New International Version" are trademarks registered in the United States Patent and Trademark Office by Biblica, Inc.™

The publisher is not responsible for websites (or their content) that are not owned by the publisher.

The Hachette Speakers Bureau provides a wide range of authors for speaking events. To find out more, go to www.hachettespeakersbureau.com or call (866) 376-6591.

Library of Congress Control Number: 2018948928

ISBNs: 978-1-5460-1080-7 (trade paperback), 978-1-5460-1079-1 (ebook)

Printed in the United States of America

LSC-C

1 3 5 7 9 10 8 6 4 2

Dedicated to my dearly departed friends
and
Don Piper Ministries Board of Directors Members
William "Sonny" Steed
Eldon Pentecost
David Gentiles
You know I'll see you at the gates

Table of Contents

THE QUESTIONS ON EVERYONE'S MINDS

WHAT DO YOU WANT YOUR LEGACY TO BE?

People I Met
At the Gates of
HEAVEN

My Story

Chapter 1

I Died and Entered Heaven

I didn't have a near-death experience (NDE).

On January 18, 1989, I died. *Literally.*

That's important for me to establish. Many books have been published since *90 Minutes in Heaven* was released in 2004. Most of them—as far as I know—told of their near-death experiences. That doesn't invalidate what happened to them, but their heavenly encounters were different.

Often those whose earthly life is ending careen down a long tunnel with a bright light at its end. That wasn't my experience. I believe that was because my death was instantaneous.

My small Ford Escort was crossing a bridge over Lake Livingston in East Texas on a cold rainy morning on my way back to Houston to speak at our evening church service. I was traveling about forty-five miles per hour when a tractor-trailer truck entered my lane at about sixty miles an hour. The semi struck me head-on. The impact was not only ghastly, but also immediately fatal.

One moment, I saw the eighteen-wheeler coming right toward me; the next moment I was standing in heaven.

In front of me stood open a beautiful gate, which looked like the inside of an oyster, sculpted from mother-of-pearl. It was one of heaven's twelve gates of pearl. And they never close!

I felt an indescribable peace as I walked toward the gate. Unlike what often happens when we gain consciousness after surgery—a bit groggy and disoriented—I didn't have to wonder where I was. I was completely awake. *As soon as I arrived, I knew.*

But there were surprises. My first was the crowd of people who suddenly surrounded me. I like to call them my personal welcoming committee. Each person was someone who had played a significant role in my life on earth. They either helped me become a Christian or they strengthened me in my growth to keep moving forward in my faith.

Joy filled their faces as they held out their arms to me. I had known each person on earth through good and bad times, and had often seen them smile. This time, each of them grinned in such a way that I thought (at least afterward), *I've never seen any of them so completely happy.*

Their greetings were heavenly and beyond human expression. Some embraced me, others shouted greetings, and all praised God for bringing me home.

As they surged toward me, I knew without question that they were there to welcome me. I felt it in every fiber of my being. The best way I can explain it is to use the word *intuitive*: knowing without being aware of how I gained that knowledge.

I didn't touch my precious greeters, whom I had loved and lost, as we think of touch. Our embrace was between two souls. It was as if my heart held each one in a holy hug. I'd been separated from some of them by more than a quarter century. Can you imagine holding a dear loved one you hadn't embraced in twenty-five years? What a joyful reunion!

As I looked at each face, I knew all of them well. Every person called me by name. And one thing became immediately clear: My presence was no accident—at least to them. They *knew* I was coming. On earth, all of us have had some sort of accident, but there are no accidents in heaven.

After I arrived, I didn't think to ask questions, such as "How did they know?" And the answers didn't matter. Their presence felt natural. In fact, everything I saw and felt seemed perfectly ordered. I marveled at the perfection of everything—people, sights, fragrances, and sounds.

And that peaceful sense of intuitively knowing stayed with me.

No one had to remind me of what they had done for me or how they had influenced me. Our "conversations" centered on their joy to see me and my excitement at being with them once again. No thought intruded into my mind about my death, my family, or anything I'd left behind. God had simply removed anything about my earthly life.

Later, I realized it was the most focused I'd ever been in my life—and it was effortless. Nothing distracted me. I was there, in the moment that seemed to have no end.

How far away was my greeting committee? I don't know. Distance seems to have no place in heaven. I saw them, took in the joy of their presence, and felt ecstasy—a sudden, intense, and all-consuming emotion—at being there.

———

Once inside heavenly territory, I didn't know if the greeting took place in four seconds or twenty minutes by earthly measurement. After my return to earth, I was told that the EMTs had declared me dead at 11:45 a.m., on the bridge. A pastor named Dick Onarecker prayed and sang a hymn in the wreckage of my car ninety minutes later at 1:15 p.m. When I speak of ninety minutes, that's conservative. Someone had to report the accident and summon the ambulance. That means my time in heaven may have been closer to two hours.

But it doesn't matter. In heaven, time doesn't exist. Everything just *is*.

After the joy-filled greetings, my welcoming committee excitedly escorted me toward one of heaven's twelve gates. I was ready to take my first step inside. I stared inside the gates of pearl, drinking in the sights before me.

That was the end of my heavenly experience.

My writing partner, who was skeptical that I had literally died when I first told him my story, became a believer when I pointed out two significant facts. First, with the severity of my later-diagnosed injuries, had I been alive, I would have bled to death. My upper left leg had exploded in the collapsing crash of my car. Four and a half inches of my femur had been ejected from my leg on impact and traveled over the railing of the bridge into the lake below. My left arm had been nearly severed and was hanging behind me in the backseat. I had many other open wounds over my face, right leg, and torso.

Second, medical experts report that four minutes is about as long as a person can survive successfully without oxygen. After six, the person becomes what one person called a "human vegetable."

Four EMTs had already pronounced me dead. Following Texas state law, they couldn't move my body until the coroner or a justice of the peace *officially* pronounced the word and completed an investigation.

I won't go into the details, which appear in *90 Minutes in Heaven*, but I understood why I wasn't allowed to enter through the gate.

Pastor Dick Onarecker, whom I hadn't known, came on the scene of the accident. He insisted on praying for me. The police officer refused because he felt the pastor would endanger himself by climbing inside the wreckage of the car with my body.

Dick insisted, "This sounds strange, but God has told me I must pray for him."

The man scoffed and said, "Sir, that man is dead. And he's been dead a long time."

"I have to pray for him. I've never done anything like this before, but I believe God wants me to pray for him."

My car was covered by a tarp with my dead body trapped inside. (Later, they brought in the Jaws of Life to cut open the mangled vehicle and take me out.) Even though I was already dead, Dick, who had a medical background, checked for a pulse but couldn't find one. He later told me that in asking God to bring me back, he prayed for what in retrospect seems strange. He prayed two distinct prayers: one, that I would have no internal injuries; and two, that there would be no brain damage.

During Dick's prayers, my spirit returned to my body. I was alive—again. God heard and answered Dick's prayers.

Dick checked my pulse again after he prayed. "He's alive! He's alive!" he shouted.

The officer didn't believe him.

"If you won't go over and check on him again," Dick cried out, "I'm going to lie down right here—right in front of this ambulance! You'll have to run over me to get me out of here."

As Dick told me the story, he said the officer shrugged and decided to humor the pastor. He called two EMTs to come over and check me.

The first EMT found a pulse.

Not only was I alive, but there was no brain injury. And despite all the physical complications that resulted, there was no internal damage, which baffled doctors who saw the accident report.

I came back because of the prayers of that pastor. And as I learned later, the petitions of many, many believers.

———————

For two years I didn't tell anyone what had happened while I lay dead on the bridge—not even my wife, Eva. The experience was too intimate, too special. And until the writing of this book, the experience of meeting those specific people at the gates of heaven was too sacred to share.

I remembered everything clearly, and sometimes, in my darkest moments, the only comfort I found was remembering in detail my heavenly experience.

I didn't taste anything in heaven, but it would have been delicious. One day we'll dine at the Lord's table and eat of the fruit trees, including the tree of life. Even now we can anticipate "tasting" heaven. Heaven is a blissful buffet for the senses, and the sensory elements I experienced are why I can remember heaven so clearly to this day.

I became instantly aware of colors that I'd never seen before, hues and shades not perceptible by earth-bound eyes. Those previously unknown aromas permeated my senses. In fact, everything about heaven pervaded me.

Certain smells trigger memories from our past. For instance, one specific brand of perfume or after-shave can cause us to remember people and events. Specific flowers' fragrances remind us of our grandma's garden or a treasured vacation spot.

One of the strongest memories I have is of the faint fragrance that permeates heaven. It took me a long time to figure out how to talk about that aroma. Then I thought of a statement in Revelation 5:8, where the Lamb clearly refers to Jesus and goes on to mention those at his throne: "Each had a harp and they were holding golden bowls full of incense, *which are the prayers of God's people*" (emphasis mine).

It makes me smile to think that the fragrance I smelled was composed of the "prayers of the saints." Add that to the smells of the aromatic tree of life, the fruit trees and their blossoms—all the glories of paradise—and the fragrance of heaven is a perfume you can't forget.

Paul writes that Christ "uses us to spread the aroma of the knowledge of him everywhere" (2 Corinthians 2:14). We are to be that lingering aroma to others through our witness, whether with words or deeds.

While we remain here on earth, we're called to be "the pleasing aroma of Christ among those who are being saved and those who are perishing" (2 Corinthians 2:15). When I think about those who influenced me, I can see that their witness is still a consistent, sweet-smelling inspiration—even now.

———◆———

Two years after the accident, I finally told my best friend, David Gentiles, about my heavenly journey and its incredible sensory offerings (though I left out the part about those who met me at the gates). He wept as I opened my heart to him. "You must tell others," he said. He urged me to tell Eva and our mutual close friend, Cliff McArdle, immediately.

"You must share this experience," Eva said after she heard my story. Later, she told me she knew something had taken place—that I had come back different, a good different—and in such a way that she couldn't explain it. She knew that the early periods of sadness and depression after surviving the accident couldn't have been only from the pain of recovery. After I told her, she understood that it was because I missed being in heaven.

Cliff responded much like David and Eva.

Although I was cautious about whom I told, to my joyful surprise, every person listened attentively with utter amazement. They didn't use the same words, but in essence, they said, "You don't think God would have allowed you to experience this if you were supposed to keep it a secret, do you?"

After repeated urging, slowly I became emboldened and opened up to individuals. Without exception, they echoed the words of David, Cliff, and Eva.

As word spread and when asked, I spoke in churches about what had happened. By then, I felt one reason God had brought me back was to share my experience, and let others know the delight and perfection of heaven. I wanted to shout, "You don't have to be afraid of death!"

I told my story in church after church or to any group who would listen. Audiences responded enthusiastically and wanted to hear more. The more I traveled, the more people pushed me to write a book about my experience—which I finally did: *90 Minutes in Heaven.*

One weekend shortly before *90 Minutes in Heaven* came out, I was out of town preaching at a church. While I was gone, Eva received thirty phone calls from pastors, inviting me to speak at their churches. Not once did I doubt that was God's leading.

From 2004 through 2015, I averaged speaking more than two hundred times a year all over the United States and various countries, especially in Europe.

But I hadn't yet told anyone about those who greeted me at the gates of heaven. I'm finally ready to share that sacred part of my story. The lives of each one of my greeters at the gates of heaven deeply impacted my life and faith. I long to live in such a way that I affect others' faith as I was affected. When those who've met me in turn do the same, they will influence generations yet to come. What a glorious legacy each one of us can leave!

———————

Heaven is a real place, and it's also a prepared place—prepared for those who follow Jesus Christ. I've dedicated my life to getting everyone I can into that perfect place because I want people to experience not only the sights, sounds, and fragrances, but the Lord Himself. He's there, waiting to welcome each one who comes to Him.

Chapter 2

My Calling

W hat qualifies me to write this book? For a long time, I wrestled with this question. Finally I simply said, "I went there and then I returned." That's my reason and my authority. After telling my story in my first book, *90 Minutes in Heaven*, I assumed that was the end. I'd told everything I needed to tell, and figured that was all people wanted to know.

But it wasn't the end.

Doors opened all over the world to speak. I could barely keep up with the requests. God called me to be a preacher, so I went.

On many nights when I hobbled into my hotel room, my ankles were so swollen I could hardly get my feet out of my shoes. Most nights I ached everywhere in my body. I chose not to use heavy medication because though it stopped the pain, it made me feel completely depleted and out of it. The horrific car accident left my body battered, covered with the scars of thirty-four surgeries due to injuries sustained in the accident.

I tell you this *not* to elicit sympathy, but to affirm I kept on for one reason: *I believed without a doubt that the Holy Spirit of God led me.* I promised the Lord, "As long as you give me life, you can use me, and when I'm done, take me back home permanently."

There are those who have been wary of me and my story. Someone even cynically suggested that I was trying to capitalize financially on my heavenly visit. I died in 1989. Had I planned to capitalize financially through telling my story, I wouldn't have waited until 2004, fifteen years later, to write my story. Neither would I have formed a nonprofit ministry to distribute funds generated from selling books and speaking about my experience. Nor would I have waited seven years after my last book[1] to write this one.

Sometimes I feel like the blind man who had his sight restored by Jesus on the Sabbath. He was interrogated by the religious leaders, who were angry that Jesus had healed someone on their sacred day of rest. They tried to get the once-blind man to say that Jesus was a terrible sinner and couldn't have healed him. The man didn't argue, and his response was simple: "One thing I do know. I was blind but now I see" (John 9:25).

That's how I feel when people want to discount my experience. I can't force them to believe. I can say only, "One thing I know: I died and now I'm alive again."

I smile sometimes when I think about that heavenly trip. Less than an hour before the accident, I had left a pastors' retreat and was on my way to speak at church that evening. A big truck ran over

---

1   Don Piper and Cecil Murphey, *Getting to Heaven: Departing Instructions for Your Life Now* (New York: Berkley Publishing Group), 2011.

my car, head-on, and killed me. Instantly, I was transported to the gates of heaven.

Obviously, I didn't stay there.

I was sent back to this life—a life filled with magnificent joy and profound pain. God didn't fully heal my body, then or later. But I found comfort in the words of Peter and John when they saw the lame man at the temple asking for alms. "Silver and gold I do not have, but what I do have I give to you" (Acts 3:6). Peter healed the man.

I can't heal anyone physically, but I can share my heart and encourage others. I'm not attempting to equate myself with the apostle Paul, but I understand what he meant when he reflected on his own heavenly experience. Paul writes of himself: "I know a man in Christ who fourteen years ago was caught up to the third heaven. Whether he was in the body or out of the body I do not know—God knows. And I know that this man...was caught up to paradise and heard inexpressible things, things that no one is permitted to tell" (2 Corinthians 12:2–4).

Luke doesn't give much backstory about Paul and skims over details about his being stoned at Lystra: "[Jews from Antioch and Iconium] stoned Paul and dragged him outside the city, thinking he was dead. But after the disciples had gathered around him, he got up and went back into the city" (Acts 14:19–20).

Did Paul die then?

It's hard for me to think that they pelted him with huge rocks, crushing every part of his body, dragged him outside the city, and not be certain he was dead. For a crowd that angry, wouldn't they have made sure he wasn't still breathing?

We don't know precisely what happened, but something powerful took place. Paul had to have been mortally wounded—crushed

and believed dead. If the rocks hadn't killed him, the rough drag-
ging would surely have finished him. After the crowd left, the
disciples came and prayed.

The left-for-dead apostle got up and went back to his ministry,
utterly undeterred by stones that bruised his body but could not
dampen his enthusiasm to share the truth that Christ can set all
people free.

That fits my definition of a miracle.

I died in a car wreck. I've published five books, including this
one, and another has been written about my experience. I take
all of that as a sure sign that the story has touched a nerve and
a need.

During the decade after *90 Minutes in Heaven* was published,
I lost track of the number of people who had NDEs and wrote
about them. I can say that in my many, many speaking engagements, I met approximately thirty people who had a true-death
experience as I did. They've chosen not to tell their stories in book
form.

One industry executive stated that my first book, *90 Minutes
in Heaven*, started a virtual renaissance in "the reality of heaven."
Millions of souls in many countries have heard me share my testimony of the remarkable visit that I made to the gates of heaven.
They've heard me discuss enduring my disappointing return to
earth and the nightmare of horrific injuries, pain, and uncertainty
that followed.

Hundreds of radio and television interviews, newspaper and
magazine articles have referred to my experience. In 2015, a

theatrical movie based on my experiences was shown across the country.

Our family never envisioned having our lives captured on the big screen. Who knew that my story would be for sale at Walmart?

As I wrote earlier, I want to be clear that I never planned to share my heavenly encounter with anyone, let alone do it publicly. But close friends and family members, whose judgment I trust more than my own, pleaded (not an exaggeration) with me to do so. I finally yielded to their counsel.

That decision changed the course of my life. After all these years, I confess I still have mixed emotions about the outcome of that decision. Travel for a survivor with such debilitating and extensive injuries as mine would never have been my choice unless prompted by the Holy Spirit.

I wouldn't do this for a living. I do it because it is a *calling*. With my own eyes and ears, I've witnessed the encouragement my account has engendered, the tears it has wiped away, and the solace it has delivered.

How am I different after my return to earth? The simple answer to that question is this: I've never been the same again. Something indescribable happened to me, and I didn't know how to explain it even to myself.

I'm hesitant to tell you the effects because I'm not a perfect man and still fail, but I can say a few things: I'm more compassionate. I care more about people. I'm more patient. Also, because I underwent thirty-four surgeries and I still live in pain, I'm much more understanding toward others who suffer.

When I've spoken with those who've had NDEs, they've tried to explain the changes that took place in them, and I can relate to these statements:

- "I feel broadened."
- "Jesus is much more real to me and has made me more faithful in reading my Bible and praying."
- "I've become more introspective and open to spiritual things."
- "Life means more to me now—and I want to relish every minute until Jesus takes me home."
- "I look forward to the day when I'll go to heaven forever."
- "My gaze lingers on a flower, a puppy, a baby, a sunrise, and more. I know that each time easily could be my last glimpse."

Not one person who has talked with me showed evidence of pride or being more "spiritual." None spoke of being perfect. Instead, many of them have spoken about a greater hunger for God and new, better goals.

Since 2004, *90 Minutes in Heaven* has sold about eight million copies. I don't intend this to be bragging, but to point to the motivation for what I do. People are buying *and* reading my words. I can't be available to speak to everyone, but when they read what I've written, that's one of the best ways I have to touch the hearts of those who don't know Jesus. Mark Batterson said it well: "For me, a book sold is not a book sold; a book sold is a prayer answered. I don't know the name and situation of every reader, but God does."

I feel a compulsion—an overwhelming drive—to reach out to others, especially those who have no relationship with Jesus Christ. I yearn for them to know my Savior.

In 2015, after the release of the movie adaptation of *90 Minutes in Heaven*, I slowed down—I truly needed it. Exhaustion and pain filled every single day. I assumed I was nearing the end of my sojourn on earth, and at age sixty-seven, I was ready to go to my eternal home.

But (obviously) God wasn't ready. Slowly excitement and joy crept back into my soul, and I *knew* I had more to offer the world. This book is a major result of that emotional and physical renewal. I'm back speaking. Will it go back to the two-hundred-plus speaking engagements each year that I did for eleven years? I don't know. I firmly believe that God does not call people to do things that He does not equip them to do. I can say only, "Lord, as You give me strength, and as You open the doors, I'm determined to serve You."

One of the major blessings in all of this is that sharing my story has brought hope to those who've lost loved ones. My experience has removed the fear and trepidation from many facing their last days on this earth.

Even after the multitude of responses that I've received since my journey to heaven and back—and they are legion—I have yet to share a detailed account of exactly whom I met at the gates of heaven:

- What were the people at the gates like?
- Why did those individuals greet me at the gates?
- Why did I come back?

This book is my response to those questions and many others.

I'm finally ready to share this story of the people who met me at the gates of heaven. The spiritual influence that each of them had on Don Piper took place long before I arrived at heaven's gates the morning of January 18, 1989. Without their combined influence, I wouldn't have made it to those pearly gates.

By sharing what I experienced, I want readers to sense the joy and perfection of heaven. And those who've put their faith in Jesus will enter into their heavenly, eternal home when this brief earthly journey is finished.

Chapter 3

Awe and Wonder

My last earthly breath was followed instantly by my first one in heaven. The apostle Paul says, speaking of himself and looking ahead to his heavenward trip: "We are confident, I say, and would prefer to be away from the body and at home with the Lord" (2 Corinthians 5:8).

Before my experience, I nodded in agreement when I read such verses. After my heavenly trip, I exclaimed, "Yes! Yes! I know!" Now I *know* what he meant. One of the most amazing realities for me was that so much of what I'd read about heaven in my Bible was *exactly* what I saw.

My first conscious moment after the crash, I was enveloped by a pure, intense, brilliant light. The apostle John wrote, "The city does not need the sun or the moon to shine on it, the glory of God gives it light, and the Lamb [Jesus] is its lamp" (Revelation 21:23). The apostle John was right. The luminescence wasn't from a sun or a moon. Heaven has no need for either.

On earth, I would have been blinded by such a powerful, concentrated light, but in heaven, my eyes changed—without effort. I was able to gaze at the brilliance without needing to look away.

As I stared at the pearl entryway, I felt as though it were a living thing, it was bathed in such brilliant light. I had never thought about whether the description of heaven in the book of Revelation was literal or figurative. Now I knew it was literal—because I arrived right at that shimmering, iridescent, animated pearly gate.

Each member of my welcoming committee was perfect in form. None bore scars or blemishes of any kind. I once heard Dr. Adrian Rogers say, "The only human-made things in heaven are the scars of Jesus." Jesus is the only resident of heaven with scars. They remain to remind us of how we are allowed entry.

Even though my welcoming committee and I moved toward the pearl gate, often it appeared as if we weren't walking. I could tell we were moving, but *how* we moved was beyond me.

Everyone there was ageless, fully restored, clad in glorious, luminescent robes. All the biblical references to clothing in heaven are of white robes, signifying that those wearing them are without sin. Even John's description of the elders in Revelation 4 says that they were clad in white robes and wearing golden crowns. Jesus refers to white garments in Revelation 3. When King Saul consulted a witch, she conjured Samuel from the dead, and he was wearing a robe (see 1 Samuel 28:14).

Many times, I've thought, *No one will have to get up in the morning and struggle over what to wear for the day. First, no one will ever get up. There's no morning and no night. And we will all be immaculately attired in resplendent, spotless robes.*

I was filled with wonder when I discovered that heaven has its own language. I communicated with those at the gates without the languages of earth, which have separated humans for millennia. Although knowledge and understanding generally proceeded without words, the few words spoken there were cherished indeed. Heaven is God's house and we will speak the language of heaven—which means there will never be misunderstandings!

I smile when I hear people remark, "I can't wait until I get to heaven, because I'm going to ask God about..."

In heaven, we'll realize the relevancy of most of our earthly questions. From the moment we arrive, we'll understand everything we need to know. All the confusion and uncertainty of this life will be gone.

Being in heaven means being with God.

Paul says it this way: "For now we see only a reflection as in a mirror; then we shall see face to face. Now I know in part; then I shall know fully, even as I am fully known" (1 Corinthians 13:12). It's a sacred reunion. Face-to-face!

———

Jesus' statement about having many rooms or mansions is true (see John 14:1–6). I saw elaborate structures that by earthly standards would qualify as mansions. Through the gates I saw magnificent buildings lining the street of gold—homes for the children of God.

On the night He was betrayed, Jesus promised His disciples, "My Father's house has many rooms; if that were not so, would I have told you that I am going there to prepare a place for you? And if I go and prepare a place for you, I will come back and take you to be with me that you may be where I am" (John 14:2–3). I'm confident we'll have places to live.

Occasionally someone will ask me why I didn't notice more detail than I did. Well, I was so focused on the reunion taking place directly in front of me that I wasn't as perceptive as I might have been during my brief time there. I had no thoughts of being sent back to earth. And for the short time I was there, I was mesmerized by the beauty and perfection all around me.

People in heaven certainly rejoice when they know any of us are coming. Occasionally, I'm asked if a loved one in heaven misses us here on earth. Here's my answer: They don't miss us. *They expect us.*

Jesus tells us in Luke 15:7 that heaven rejoices every time someone here makes a reservation to go there. When we profess Christ as Savior, our names are recorded in the Lamb's Book of Life, according to Revelation 21:23—God's reservation list. The Bible urges believers to "rejoice, that our names are written in heaven" (Luke 10:20).

For them, time doesn't pass. Although decades may lapse here on earth after we're temporarily separated from them, we shall join them "in the twinkling of an eye" (1 Corinthians 15:52).

Wouldn't it be surprising otherwise? Moses and Elijah, who had long since departed this earth, were recognized at the transfiguration (Matthew 17:3–4). King David believed that he would see his son after his baby died, even saying, "I will go to him" (2 Samuel 12:23).

"We shall be like him, for we shall see him as he is" (1 John 3:2). After His resurrection, Jesus showed Himself to His disciples and they recognized Him. "[Jesus] appeared to more than five hundred of the brothers and sisters at the same time, most of them are still living..." (1 Corinthians 15:6).

Matthew records what happened when Jesus died on the cross. One of the amazing facts states, "The bodies of many holy people who had died were raised to life. They came out of the tombs after Jesus' resurrection and went into the holy city and appeared to many people" (Matthew 27:52). Implicit in that statement is that their families and friends recognized them. "And just as we have borne the likeness of the earthly man, so shall we bear the likeness of the heavenly man" (1 Corinthians 15:49).

Rather than rejoice so much in the reunion, which was splendid in itself, my friends were rejoicing that God had allowed them to be forever in His presence. I was filled with overwhelming gratitude as I got ready to step forward to enter the place I had preached about for so many years. It was more than my senses could take in.

Beyond my greeters, I could see through the gate. Here are a few things I noticed, and they were as the Bible depicts them:

- The entrance is narrow (Matthew 7:13).
- The walls of the city are thick (Revelation 21:17).
- A great golden boulevard bisects the city (Revelation 21:21).
- A river flows down the street (Revelation 22:1–2).
- The tree of life stands by the river, bearing fruit, not forbidden, but accessible (Revelation 22:2). (Evidence that we will eat, not for sustenance, but fellowship.)
- Magnificent structures line the street, dwellings for the redeemed (John 14:2).

As I wrote the above, I wished I could shout to each one of you disciples of Jesus: "You're going to love it!" One compelling reason for my hesitancy about sharing my heavenly visit is that I knew I would have to use earthly words. None are adequate.

As I peered inside the tall gates, in the center of the city was a pinnacle. Beyond even the brilliant radiance at the gates, the glow was luminescent. There were thrones just as Stephen saw in Acts 7. I knew that this is where the great God of all creation and His dear Son reign over the kingdom (see Revelation 22:3).

Without hesitation, I eagerly wanted to enter the doorway, pass through the massive walls, tread the golden boulevard, and climb the gentle mount. Although I didn't see Him, I *knew* that, once inside, just as Revelation 21 states three times, I would be "with Him." I believe that is the most glorious event of the holiest place—being with God in heaven—even superseding the brilliant light I encountered at the gates. I would fall at the feet of the Lord of all creation and shout, "Thank you for letting me be here!"

I moved forward to do just that. My welcoming committee—those dear people who helped me get to heaven or encouraged me to pursue the Christian life—parted to give me free access.

———————

Beyond my reunion with my loved ones, the two things that forever touched me at the gates of heaven were angels and music.

First, angels were everywhere and many of them hovered about me when I arrived. I fully expected to hear their voices in heaven as mentioned in Revelation 5:11. And I did. But the greater blessing I received was hearing the soothing, holy *whoosh* of their wings. Angels, God's great messengers and servants, come in many forms. All are magnificent beings. Some have multiple wings; others have only two wings; still others appear without wings.

The only comparable sound I've ever heard to the *whooshing* sound of the wings of angels was stumbling upon a covey of birds in the woods as a boy. In heaven, I heard the wings of angels. In quiet moments of reflection back here on earth, I can still hear them. That's an enormously comforting and encouraging sound. I can't wait to hear them again. God knows I want everyone here to hear them.

Second, as I approached the portal of glory, my soul was utterly flooded with music. God not only gave us music, but He must be enthusiastic about it, because the melodies are exceedingly prevalent in heaven. Job 38:7 records that music began at the creation, "when the morning stars sang together and all the angels shouted for joy." Though music is mentioned in the Bible, before my visit to heaven, I hadn't thought much about heavenly music. It's a multitude of glorious melodies, all praising God. Despite what seemed to be thousands of songs being offered up simultaneously, there was no chaos, no dissonance. I could easily distinguish each one of them then, and I can still recall them now.

After I began to speak publicly about my experience, seminary music professors, musicians, and singers contacted me over these three decades to seek greater understanding of the music of heaven. Seldom does any music like the songs of heaven occur here on earth—earthly songs simply pale in comparison.

King David was a gifted musician, composer, and purveyor of songs for the glory of God. Instruments and music mentioned in the Bible include trumpets, harps, flutes, lutes, pipes (where my surname originated), tambourines, zithers, rams' horns, cymbals, lyres, gongs, psalms, songs, and choirs. I sensed that other instruments I'd never seen or heard before were part of the heavenly harmony.

"The sound I heard was like that of harpists playing their harps. And they sang a new song before the throne" (Revelation 14:2–3). Revelation 5:12–14 declares, "Worthy is the Lamb...to receive praise." God loves to hear His children praise Him with music.

I heard thousands of songs at the gates of heaven. All of them were sung simultaneously to God without chaos because they were symbiotic. The different tunes and instruments flowed together. Yet amazingly, I could distinguish each one of them with my heavenly ears.

Soaring above that tapestry of music was one distinctive song: "Holy, Holy, Holy."

The songs infused my soul. Of all the things I experienced in heaven, the music is the one I carry with me even today. I can close my eyes and still hear the heavenly melodies. I wish everyone could hear them. But that's reserved for God's people, in God's place.

Here on earth, it's been an enormous honor to be in the presence of worship experiences all over the world. Some of those worship services were held in soaring cathedrals with unsurpassed acoustics. Others in old barns without the benefit of electricity to power sound systems or instruments. I've worshiped in tents, in tiny clapboard buildings, in a clearing in the woods, school auditoriums, and houses of worship of every conceivable denomination in Christendom.

Two truths have emerged for me: One, I'm not the object of the worship. Though we *offer* the worship, God is the object of it. God alone is worthy of our worship and praise. But I do get to participate in and experience it. Two, God receives it and loves it—whether sung in English, Swahili, German, Russian, Korean, or sign language. God understands the words and the heart behind the words and music.

I didn't understand a word the worshipers offered in a barn in Norway or the Sioux at a powwow on the Fort Peck Reservation in Montana, but they were for the ears of God. I've happily heard anointed music all over earth. What a blessing. But the music in heaven? Well, that's heavenly! And we'll get to hear it forever there.

Saturated with heavenly melodies, surrounded by angelic hosts, greeted by precious people whom I'd loved and lost, I was ready to enter the great gates.

As I crossed God's "front porch" and entered the threshold of glory, everything stopped.

Instantly, I was in utter darkness and complete silence. Gasping for words, I tried to verbalize, "What happened? I've only just arrived!"

Out of the void I heard a voice. This time it wasn't in front of me the way it had been in heaven. This voice came out of darkness, not from light. Although I didn't recognize the source, I later learned it was the dedicated preacher led by God to pray over my dead body under a tarp in the wreckage of my car. His hand was on my battered body and he was pleading with God to spare me, even heal me.

He was singing "What a Friend We Have in Jesus." As I heard the words, I joined him in singing.

Then immediately I was back on earth, my body shattered and hardly recognizable. Before the pain set in, a wave of depression came over me. *Why didn't God let me stay? Why did I have to return to earth?*

I experienced pain beyond anything that I could have ever imagined, followed by years of agonizing recovery. I endured thirty-four major surgeries and years of hospitalization, therapy, and rehabilitation. But mostly, I faced this question every single day: *Why did God allow me a glimpse of heaven and then take that away from me?*

In the months after the accident, I battled severe depression—

some surely came from the constant daily pain, but the worst was my disappointment about being alive. *Why, God? Why did you send me back into this pain-filled body? Why did I get a glimpse of heaven only to have you send me back to earth with a broken body?*

Almost thirty years later, my answer is simple: It happened so that I might confirm to all who will listen that *heaven is real*, and proclaim to the world, *Jesus is the way to heaven.*

One lesson from my brief trip has convinced me that we, as followers of Jesus Christ, are here on earth to help everyone else get to heaven. When I speak and teach, I urge my audience to be sure they have their eternal reservations. And once that's settled, they need to share the wonderful news with others.

I think of the words of Jesus to His followers: "Whoever acknowledges me before others, I will also acknowledge before my Father in heaven" (Matthew 10:32).

"Ask yourselves," I often say when I speak, "who will be in heaven because of me? My lifestyle? My prayers?"

I won't meet everyone on earth, but I earnestly desire to see as many as possible at the gates of glory. Only then will we realize our complete spiritual fulfillment. Only there will we be free from pain, uncertainty, and death.

Since my return to earth, I've found rich meaning in the words of Peter: "Praise be to the God and Father of our Lord Jesus Christ! In his great mercy he has given us new birth into a living hope through the resurrection of Jesus Christ from the dead, and into an inheritance that can never perish, spoil, or fade" (1 Peter 1:3–4).

For me, the best part of Peter's message is what follows: "This inheritance is kept in heaven for you, who through faith are shielded by God's power until the coming of the salvation that is ready to be revealed in the last time. In all of this you greatly rejoice, though now for a little while you may have had to suffer grief in all kinds of trials. These have come so that your faith—of greater worth than gold, which perishes even though refined by fire—may be proved genuine and may result in praise, glory and honor when Jesus Christ is revealed" (verses 4–7).

Verses 8 and 9, even though the language is archaic in the King James Version, speaks strongly to me: "Whom having not seen, ye love; in whom, though now ye see him not, yet believing, ye rejoice with joy unspeakable and full of glory."

Joy unspeakable. Full of glory. Truly the best, yet fully inadequate, words I can use.

No matter how joyful your life may be now, if heaven is your destination, one day you *will* rejoice with joy unspeakable.

My Welcoming Committee

Chapter 4

My Influencers

None of those in my welcoming committee had been perfect humans. Like the rest of us, they had their own strengths and weaknesses, talents, and foibles. What they did possess was an abiding love for people and a deep desire to see that those not ready for heaven would come to know how to get there.

While still on earth, each of those who greeted me at the gates brought their passions and actions into my life so that I might know about heaven and desire to go there. They shared Jesus with me in deeds, words, and outlook. Sometimes, I think of myself as the by-product of their faith and faithfulness.

I can't begin to calculate the likelihood that I could have come to know Jesus without first knowing and being influenced by the people who met me at the gates of heaven. Their words and deeds had a direct and unmistakable impact on my coming to know Christ at the age of sixteen and growing as a follower.

Jesus loved me so much that He gave His life for me so that I could become eligible for heaven; my welcoming committee loved me so much that they did what they needed to do for me to make a reservation. Granted, many have influenced me for Jesus since my accident and still do. Hallelujah! I'll see them when I'm home for good.

At the time I met those glorious, radiant people at the gates of heaven, I didn't realize the full significance of the reason those specific individuals were there. I was so filled with joy and peace that I didn't think to ask about it. I'm not certain that asking questions is ever necessary in heaven.

But I knew two things: *I was home.* And I wanted to stay.

I was exactly where I belonged, and they were obviously there to joyfully, with great excitement, escort me through the gates of heaven.

In the following chapters, it's impossible (and probably unneeded) for me to mention every person at the gate. I've chosen to tell you only about a representative handful. Most of them had some responsibility in my having a reserved place in heaven. Others influenced me in special, significantly spiritual ways following my salvation experience.

I believe you'll fall in love with them just as I have.

Chapter 5

Jan Cowart

In the sweltering summer of 1966, I was sixteen years old, dressed in shorts, relaxed, and watching TV. The doorbell rang, and Mother answered the door. Seconds later she said, "Some people are here to see you."

"Who are they?"

"I think they're from some church."

I was surprised to have them visit and to ask for me. "Really?"

"There are three of them and they look like they're about your age."

My family didn't go to church in those days, so I wondered why they had come to see me. I hurriedly put on a shirt and shoes. I was excited that kids my own age would visit. My heart was racing at the thought of meeting kids from a church. No one from any church had ever come to our house. Occasionally, a neighbor casually invited me to a service or a special event where they worshiped, but that was it.

My mother invited the teens to sit and wait for me. Nervously, I walked into the living room, where they sat. Two girls and one guy. Even though they obviously knew who I was, I said, "Hi, I'm Don, pleased to meet you. Thanks for coming."

I especially remembered and liked Jan Cowart. We hadn't met, but I knew who she was; we were both rising juniors at Bossier High School in Bossier City, Louisiana. The other two teens were students at our archrival, Airline High School.

Jan was cute, charming, soft-spoken, with a stylish bob. Her dark brown eyes twinkled behind her horn-rimmed glasses. She flashed an expansive smile accompanied by a sweet schoolgirl giggle. After we were better acquainted, I considered her one of the smartest girls I knew.

The second girl was Carmen. I had been introduced to her once, although I didn't think she remembered me. She wore pointy eyeglasses, was friendly, and smiled often.

The guy introduced himself as Barry, and just from his looks, anyone would know he was a jock—a large, muscular kid with a firm handshake and a friendly grin.

We looked awkwardly at one another, followed by a short silence and a little throat-clearing. "We would like to invite you to visit our church," Barry said. "We have a great youth group at First Baptist and we think you'd really like it."

"We have all kinds of activities and fellowships," Jan said. "You already know some of the kids in our group."

"We'd love to have you," Carmen added.

I was immediately impressed that young people my age would take time out of their summer vacation to come to my home and personally extend an invitation to their church. As I remember, they stayed perhaps less than fifteen minutes, but it was enough.

"I'll be there Sunday," I promised.

"Wonderful," one of them said, and all three made it clear that they'd watch for me on Sunday.

Only later would I realize that although they were excited about inviting me to their church service, I was even more enthusiastic about attending it. They came on Thursday, and for the days until Sunday, I eagerly (and anxiously) planned to be there. I'd been to that church a few times when I was nine or ten years old. That was because my grandmother taught a children's Bible study there. As a child, I attended the church's vacation Bible schools during the summer. One year, I made some kind of artwork with Popsicle sticks, which my mother hung on the door of the refrigerator.

My father was a career man with the US Army. That meant that our family lived a nomadic life, was transferred often, and we weren't regular churchgoing people. Because of being an army brat all my life, I was tired of constantly being the new kid every place my dad was sent.

Dad had recently retired, and my parents bought a permanent home in Bossier City, Louisiana. For the first time in my life, I knew we wouldn't move within two years. I hardly knew any kids at school, so I was highly enthusiastic about making friends.

That probably made me more than normally receptive that Carmen, Jan, and Barry had thoughtfully visited me in my own house and invited me to God's house.

Something special happened to me. I kept reminding myself, they came to see *me*. Just that thought made me feel exceptional to have my peers show that kind of interest. Like any teen, I wanted to be with others my own age.

That Sunday morning, which would be life-changing, I borrowed my mother's car keys and drove to First Baptist. Once there,

I followed the directions my visitors had given me. Easily, I found the room where I was told their Sunday school class met.

Taking a deep breath, I crossed the threshold of the sophomore Bible study classroom looking for my new friends.

"You came!" Jan called out, smiling and moving toward me as soon as I entered the room.

"Just like you promised," Carmen said.

"We get a lot of promises when we visit," Barry said, "but not many of them follow through!"

I'm not sure who was the most excited that Sunday morning in 1966: me, at the prospect of becoming a part of a group like theirs; or the three kids who'd invited me, because they had asked someone to church who not only promised to come but actually showed up.

During the following months, I faithfully attended church and came to know my three inviters well. Because Jan and I attended the same school, we had more opportunities for interaction. I'm certain that I could have become closer friends with Carmen and Barry had we attended the same high school. Jan and I also shared numerous interests at Bossier High. Both of us were nominated for the state Leadership Conference at LSU, another statewide honor called Pelican State, and the National Honor Society.

Jan became editor of the student newspaper and a member of the Chemistry Club, the Physics Club, was president of the Future Homemakers of America, and was inducted into Quill and Scroll, the national honor society for journalism.

I was the president of the National Forensic League (debate club), the National Thespians Society (drama club), and a student council member. Looking back, we were almost complete nerds, but we reveled in our nerdiness, reminding ourselves that we were *in* the world, but not *of* the world. It took me a few months to grasp that concept.

We worked together on many school projects and faithfully attended youth meetings and Bible studies. I loved seeing Jan's smiling face in the halls of school or in an organization meeting when she walked through the door.

In fact, we eventually dated for several months. I'm not sure why we didn't continue, except that both of us realized we were good friends, but there wasn't any long-term romantic interest.

I learned that Jan and her older brother, Richard, had been adopted as young children by two wonderful members of First Baptist, Leo and Ethel Cowart. Consequently, they grew up at First Baptist. Jan was a deeply devoted Christian, and one of the most authentic disciples I've ever known. Her brother had been called into the ministry and was studying at a seminary in Kentucky.

Back in the 1960s, Christian young people often had get-togethers at the homes of their parents after Sunday evening services, which we called fellowships. Those informal parties were where I got to know the Cowarts well. They liked me as much as I liked them, and before long, I began to receive regular invitations to their home for dinner. Those were exceptional events considering Jan majored in home economics in high school. She was already a fabulous cook.

Although I soon discovered that cooking well doesn't always mean the diners enjoy the dinner. One of the few vegetables I don't care for is asparagus. One night the main course at the Cowarts' house consisted of an asparagus casserole. While I'm certain that it was quite tasty to many, I could have been nominated for an Oscar for the performance that I gave eating and appearing to enjoy *two* helpings of asparagus casserole. Ah, the price of courtship.

Two of my all-time favorite movies are *Gone with the Wind* and Franco Zeffirelli's *Romeo and Juliet*. I saw both films on a date with Jan Cowart at the glorious Strand Theatre in downtown Shreveport. In addition to remembering the Montagues and Capulets, as well as Scarlett and Rhett, I cherished the memory of Jan Cowart and the tears we shed into our popcorn.

Because of her loving influence, by the spring of our junior year, I knew that I wanted what Jan, Carmen, and Barry had in their hearts. Like them, I wanted Christ as my Savior. Frequently, I asked them questions about Jesus. To their credit, they gave me simple answers and never pushed me. I'm glad no one kept urging me to become a believer. Yet I wanted to know more; I studied about Jesus every opportunity I had.

After a few months, I began to read the Bible every day, starting with Genesis all the way through Revelation. And even though I didn't always understand what I was reading, I went from cover to cover with passion.

One Sunday after service, I talked with my Sunday school teacher, Joe Cobb. "I've been coming here for months now," I said. "I want to know Jesus the way you and others do."

Joe smiled, obviously pleased that I would ask. I told Jan as well. Both Jan and Joe suggested that I meet with the youth pastor of the church, Tom Cole.

That was fine with me; I had come to respect and admire Tom a great deal and considered Joe and Jan's suggestion as good counsel.

I called Tom and he agreed to meet with me in my home the next afternoon after school. He came just as he'd promised, and I was excited to see him at the door. He sat on the same brown brocade couch in the same living room where Jan, Barry, and Carmen had once invited me to church.

Tom explained what it meant for me to become a Christian, and once assured of my sincerity, he led me in prayer, and I committed my life to Jesus Christ. He told me that it was a glorious experience to make a private decision but that I should want others to know as well. And I was happy to do that.

The next Sunday morning, as I had been encouraged by Tom, I walked forward during the invitation time (what they referred to as an altar call) at Bossier City's First Baptist Church. I was greeted by our pastor, Dr. Damon Vaughn. I told him of my newfound faith. He expressed great delight with my decision and made it known to the entire church family that I was now one of them, a sinner saved by grace. Jesus was *my* Savior. First Baptist became *my* church and the members *my* spiritual family.

After the service, the first people coming to congratulate me were Joe Cobb, Tom Cole, Barry, Carmen, and Jan. They were also present two weeks later when I was baptized. Their genuine happiness for me was palpable—almost as if they were reliving their own salvation experiences through my decision and my baptism.

Before Jan, Carmen, Barry, and I went off to college in 1968, we had many fine moments of Christian fellowship at First Baptist—Bible studies, after-church fellowships, youth retreats, pizza parties, group dates, and Sunday afternoon touch football games. My life wouldn't have been the same without that foundation.

I lost track of Carmen soon after we started college. I heard that she was happily married, had become a mother, and lived not far from Bossier City, across the state line in East Texas, but I never saw her again.

Barry went to college on an athletic scholarship to play football. He later married and had several children, including at least three sons, and each played quarterback for the US Air Force Academy. The last time I spoke to Barry, he had been named head football coach and athletic director for a large Christian school in the Dallas, Texas, area.

―――――

Following my salvation decision, no one was more supportive than Jan. Through good times and bad, she always seemed to have a good word for me. She encouraged me when I was down, never condescending or judgmental, and she lovingly warned me if she felt I was getting off track in my Christian walk.

From the beginning of my faith journey through my growth as a faithful follower of Christ, I couldn't have had a more genuinely faithful friend. Although our romantic relationship didn't continue through our senior year, I cherished her friendship and greatly admired her unwavering faith in God.

After college, our paths took us in different directions. But I always smiled when I thought of Jan; some people just do that to me. It wasn't only the many wonderful times that we had at church or on dates. Jan Cowart played a crucial part in my spiritual walk with the Lord.

Only God knows what would have happened during the later days of my high school career and in college had not three freshly scrubbed and nervous young people shown up at my door on Fullilove Drive one summer afternoon and invited me to their church.

Ten years later, my heart sank when I heard of her passing. Jan, a lifelong Type 1 diabetic, had fought the disease courageously, until it took her life at the youthful age of only twenty-eight. She had always been candid with me about her dependence on daily insulin injections. Jan had married after graduating from college, though she left behind no children. She was one of the kindest, most caring, loyal friends I've ever known.

In heaven, Jan was one of the first ones to reach me. Although no words were spoken, I can tell you the feelings and the emotions I experienced and what words would have passed between us.

"Welcome home, Don!" She would have giggled as she often had on earth, just the way she had the first time I met her.

Two decades later, she was once again welcoming me—this time at heaven's gates. She had happily embraced me at church on the morning that I made my decision for Christ known. She joyfully hugged me at the gates of heaven. Her influence had been so significant to my knowing Christ.

Sometimes I'm still amazed at that reality: Jan Cowart knew that I was coming that day and she was there to meet me.

I don't know *how* she and the others knew that I would arrive at that moment—and that's not important. *They knew. They were ready for me.*

Jan deserved to be there with the bevy of greeters because she, more than anyone else, helped me get there. She quietly guided me in my spiritual growth, and I can never be thankful enough.

In all honesty, seeing Jan again at heaven's gate was just too sacred to share before now. In all my speaking around the world, I've never mentioned her.

Perhaps the circumstances of her earthly life and death have been too painful to relive. In 1972, Jan's brother, Richard, and his pregnant wife (both twenty-five years old) were killed in a horrible car accident coming home from seminary. Jan's own earthly existence ended in 1978. Brother and sister, lovingly adopted as children by the kindly Cowarts, were together again. They were all laid to rest at Shreveport's Greenwood Cemetery before they turned thirty years old.

Now I believe it's time for me to open up and tell about her influence, if only to help you see the part you need to play in leading others to Christ.

None of us comes to God alone—all of us have others who encouraged, nudged, or exhorted us to turn to God. Some of them lived the life that honored the Savior even though their words may have been few or their time on earth had been brief.

If we're believers, not only can we know that heaven awaits us, but we can also know that we'll have a personal welcoming committee! They'll have gone there before us and met their own special cloud of witnesses. The "baton" of salvation is passed from one soul to the next. And the next.

Chapter 6

Mike Wood

On November 17, 1968, the *Shreveport Times* published a photo of Mike Wood with four other area athletes who were starters for the "Baby Bengals" (the nickname for LSU's freshmen football team). Mike stood in the center, clearly bigger than the other uniformed North Louisiana football players. I saw the *Times* photo and felt proud that he was doing so well.

His picture was back in the paper ten days later. This time it was in the obituaries.

I want to tell you about that wonderful guy. Although Mike Wood and I went to the same school and he was a member of First Baptist Church, our only interactions were in classes that we shared, organizations where we served, or a nod when we passed in the hall. I definitely knew who he was; but then, everybody knew Mike Wood.

For one thing, he was a large kid, tall and big—hard to miss, and handsome. The girls were completely enamored of him and the boys wanted to be like him. To top it off, he was one of the most well-adjusted teens I'd ever known.

I was known to say, "Mike has the kind of smile that lights up a room and a grin that would defrost a refrigerator."

I was a borderline nerdy kid. I liked public speaking, and English was a favorite subject. More important, I wasn't an athlete. I ran track and was in good physical shape, but no one ever called me a jock. I spent so much of my time engaged in the debate club and the theater group, I didn't have energy for the incredible amount of time it took to be an athlete. Most of my extracurricular activities involved suits and ties.

By contrast, Mike was an amazing athlete. He was the complete package—humble, yet popular; friendly, and soft-spoken. He exhibited many enviable traits, yet his faith in Christ was evident, which was unique for somebody as popular as he was. Mike quietly and with assurance spoke about his faith whenever he could.

I think it's often harder to minister to the up-and-out than to the down-and-out. They have no sense of need. With all that Mike had going for him: his looks, his athletic ability, and his girlfriend—I mean, that's what kids look for when they're that age—why would he need the Lord?

But despite his size and popularity, Mike didn't intimidate anyone, and yet no one ever argued with him when he spoke about Jesus. He was so open and forthright, I don't think anyone saw it as a sales pitch. Mike was genuine. And it showed. He certainly didn't seem like he needed anything, but then, he already had Jesus. And he was unapologetic about it.

His relationship with the Savior was what made Mike the way he was. I can honestly say I never once saw him behave in an un-Christian way. He wasn't perfect—but Mike was certainly farther along the spiritual path than the rest of us.

He allowed his life on and off the sports field to be a witness.

When we were both sophomores, Mike started dating Pat White, the head drum majorette of the Bossier High School marching band. She was petite, a cute blonde, and Mike was dark-haired and a foot taller than Pat. They were like the leads in a teenage movie.

Pat fell for him, and apparently, Mike loved her. Truthfully, I never met anyone who didn't like Mike. His parents adored him, and it was obvious he felt loved and secure. The school coaches thought he was wonderful. Why wouldn't they? Mike lettered in four sports, and somehow still remained humble.

During the years I was in high school, Shreveport, Louisiana, was nicknamed the quarterback factory because Joe Ferguson was playing at our rival, Woodlawn High School. He went on to become a quarterback in the NFL for the Buffalo Bills.

On any given Sunday, Joe Ferguson's predecessor at Woodlawn, Terry Bradshaw, and other NFL quarterbacks from North Louisiana, including James Harris, Bert Jones, Doug Williams, and David Woodley, would be slinging passes in the NFL—all from North Louisiana.

We at Bossier High School had stiff competition in sports from students who went on to have incredible careers. I'm sure that had Mike lived, his football career would have been outstanding.

———

I never expected to meet Mike, let alone become his friend. I believed I wasn't in his league, and our worlds were too different. Mike and I met when I was a sophomore. My family moved to his town after my dad retired from the US Army and came home from Vietnam.

One day Mike and Pat invited me to sit with them at their lunch table. For kids like me who were new at the school, it was a big deal to feel welcomed. I don't know why they welcomed me, but they included me and considered me one of them. I felt humbled to be included as a friend of theirs, stunned really that they would reach out to me. After we became friends, Mike told me he had been a Christian since childhood.

We never had long to eat at school and we couldn't leave the campus, but since the meals were pretty good, it was fine. But as good as the meals were, they were never enough for a growing boy like Mike. I learned not to sit next to him. Whenever I became involved in a conversation with someone else and looked away, Mike would stab the chicken or beef off my plate. After quickly devouring it, he'd smile.

I knew it was all in fun and it became a joke at our table to protect our plate from Mike's oversized hunger.

———————◆———————

Our Sunday school teacher at First Baptist, Joe Cobb, owned Cobb's Barbeque. We had fellowship meetings after church at his house for his Sunday school class of eleventh-grade boys—perhaps fifteen of us. Joe would bring home food from the restaurant: ham, brisket, potato salad, coleslaw, and especially banana pudding. Of course, when Joe had us over, it was a joyous thing. Rarely was any food left—especially the evenings Mike attended. I couldn't wrap my brain around the quantities of food that kid could consume while never putting on a pound.

Some of my best memories from my teen years were with those young people at church, learning about Jesus, growing and fellowshipping with them at school and church. Whenever Mike was present, he would encourage me to read my Bible and pray. I warmly remember the times we went around our Sunday school class and each of us read aloud a verse of Scripture. A number of us sixteen-year-old guys squirmed and haltingly read our verse, sometimes struggling with the names of little-known biblical characters. But when it was Mike's turn, he read flawlessly and smiled, as if to say, "I did it." And he did.

The Sunday I walked down the aisle at church to proclaim my faith in Jesus Christ, Mike hurried to greet me. And he was present when I was baptized. I'm so grateful that whenever I needed a friend or someone to talk to, Mike was there, ready to listen intently, letting me know he cared. He wasn't focused on what he was going to say when I paused. He was focused on me. He was a kid of few words, but when he spoke, it was heartfelt and caring.

High school ended for both of us in 1968. On a crisp May evening we received our diplomas on the same football field where Mike had so often displayed his amazing athletic skills. And as typical as it is when that happens, all of us were never together in the same town again.

We didn't know we wouldn't *see* each other again.

Mike received a full scholarship to play football at LSU at Baton Rouge. In those days, college freshmen weren't allowed to play on the varsity football team. But Mike was a starter for the freshman team, which was a tribute to his ability. Word came back that he was one of the best.

I'd planned to enlist in the Army after graduation and serve like my father before me—putting in my twenty years. Instead, my father urged me to go to college. Even though he came from a long line of military people going all the way back to the siege at Vicksburg in the Civil War (my great-great-great-great-grandfather Israel Piper fell on that battlefield, fighting for the 99th Illinois Infantry), he was adamant. "No, son, no," Dad said. He had retired in the early days of the war in Southeast Asia. He knew too much about Vietnam. He came home from there with medals and horrifying memories. And he knew the dangers I'd face. "Stay in college and get your education."

I felt disappointed, since I'd been certain he would be proud of me for volunteering.

Dad then appealed to my pride: "You'll be the first in our family to receive a college degree. After you finish, if you still want to go into the Army, I guess it'll be okay."

I honored my dad's wish and enrolled at LSU Shreveport. After one year, I transferred to LSU's main campus in Baton Rouge.

———

Six months after high school graduation, I was sitting in our den when the phone rang. "It's for you," my mother said. "Whoever it is sounds upset."

"This is Jan Cowart and I have some very bad news." Her voice broke and she blurted out, "Mike Wood is dead!"

"If this is a joke, it's not a good one," I said, already reeling in pain and confusion. I collapsed into the nearest chair.

"It's not a joke." Between tears, Jan filled me in on the details of what had happened on Barksdale Boulevard in Bossier City. At 8:10 p.m. on November 27, 1968, the day before Thanksgiving, Mike was in a pickup truck with his best friend's dad, Mr. Allen. They had gone hunting, killed a deer, and were taking it to Peterson's Grocery, a meat processor on Barksdale Boulevard. As Mr. Allen started to cross a highway to reach the meat processor, they were struck broadside by a truck.

I don't think anybody knows exactly what happened.

Mike died instantly. Mr. Allen sustained non-life-threatening injuries.

Later, I thought, *My big, strong friend had been hit so many times by tackles playing football, but he was no match for tons of steel and glass.*

I had no way to know that slightly more than twenty years later, the same thing would happen to me.

The day after she gave me the news of Mike's death, Jan and I decided to go to his house. We had zero experience in such situations. We also hadn't thought about others going, too, and as we got close, I couldn't find a parking space anywhere near his house. Of course, everybody in the neighborhood knew what had happened. I mean, Mike was a shining star of that city, and now he was gone. Finally, I found a spot three blocks away.

The front door was propped open; people were coming and going. Mike's two younger brothers, Larry and Kevin, were sitting in the front, ashen-faced and staring off into space. They only nodded when anyone addressed them.

Jan and I stepped inside and Mike's parents were sitting in chairs. They seemed lost in their pain. Mrs. Wood sniffled occasionally and automatically wiped her eyes with the handkerchief she held in her right hand. Mike's dad acknowledged guests but didn't seem able to speak.

Jan and I stood in line, and when our turn came, we tried to say a few comforting words. I can't remember what I said, but my words came from a grief-stricken heart. I doubt that anything registered with either parent.

To our left and down a hallway a muffled wailing came from the back of the house. Jan and I carefully brushed past the people standing in the hallway and went to the source of the sobbing.

Mike's best friend from childhood, Don Allen, lay on Mike's bed groaning as if he were in deep pain. Brokenhearted. Devastated. It seemed to me that he had cried so much, no more tears would come, but the muffled whimpering and moaning cut to my heart.

Without saying a word, I closed the door softly. Jan and I both felt crushed and overwhelmed. In fact, for the next two days, everything was a blur of tears and wordless groaning.

———◆———

The funeral turned out to be massive, presided over by our pastor, Dr. Damon Vaughn. The room was filled with former classmates and members of our youth group. Nearly twice as many people came as could fit inside the Rose-Neath Funeral Home. The entire LSU football coaching staff stood against the side wall because they didn't want to take up seats. Many mourners had to stand outside.

Mike's mom and dad, his two brothers, Pat White, and Don Allen sat quietly, pale and crestfallen.

In an unexplainable way, as I sat there, for the first time I was confronted with my own mortality. I wondered what it would mean if my lifeless body lay in that casket. Then I tried to imagine what Mike's life would have been like had he lived longer.

After the funeral, we followed an enormous procession of cars to his gravesite. Today, fifty years later, his brown granite gravestone still shines, reminding those who knew him that he was a rock. "MICHAEL DAVID WOOD," it reads, "1950–1968." Etched across the bottom are the opening words of Psalm 121: "I WILL LIFT UP MINE EYES UNTO THE HILLS."

The night after the funeral, I lay in bed, closed my eyes, and remembered Mike's infectious smile. Unable to sleep, I flipped through the pages of our 1968 yearbook, *Les Mémoires*. I stared at his photograph, seeing Mike frozen in time, shooting hoops, catching passes, and smiling from those pages. He will forever be eighteen.

Ten years after I got the call from Jan Cowart about Mike's death, she joined our mutual friend in glory. Nothing will ever separate them again.

———◆———

Mike represented not just physical strength but strength of character. That may not sound like a big deal, but as a teenager, it was huge. It impressed me for the rest of my life. He had become a Christian long before I did and remained faithful. His life was not long, like a comet streaking across the sky.

Today, less than two miles from the accident site, a beautiful city park stands in our hometown of Bossier City filled with towering pecan trees, a jogging track, Frisbee golf, playgrounds, picnic tables, tennis courts, and an Olympic-size swimming pool. Driving down into the pastoral park, I passed through a wrought-iron gate inscribed with these words:

Mike Wood Memorial Park

His hometown hadn't forgotten a favorite son.

———◆———

When our class of '68 gathered for its tenth anniversary, several classmates were gone, killed in Vietnam, American heroes. But also heartbreaking was the loss of football player and friend Mike Wood. All of them gone, but never forgotten.

I was the master of ceremonies at the reunion. In deep solemnity, we lit candles for the ones we knew who had passed away. Then, I read the names of our dearly departed classmates aloud. When I came to Mike's name, memories flooded back—some precious, some very painful.

———◆———

In 1989, when I stood in front of the gates of heaven, Mike and Jan, smiling radiantly, held out their arms to me. They were both expecting me, and greeted me joyfully. Three of us were in that same graduating class in 1968, and now we had graduated to the gates of heaven. Without a doubt, heaven's reunion is the most incomparable reunion of all.

Mike was happier in heaven than I had ever seen him on earth. He greeted me with the same lovable grin that we all enjoyed here on earth, except it was even more expansive, joy spread across his face.

I stared into his joyous, life-filled countenance. For the first time, I think I fully understood Paul's words, when he referred to "the peace of God, which transcends all understanding" (Philippians 4:7). Without saying anything, Mike radiated a joy that could find no human words to express. And as he focused on me, his delight in seeing and welcoming me was greater than any expression

I had ever seen on his naturally happy face. His arms embraced and welcomed me—a friend, an earthly brother—and pointed toward the entrance to our heavenly home.

Instead of a football jersey, at heaven's gate his lanky form was clad in an amazingly brilliant robe. Everybody wore one. I looked down at myself and saw that I was dressed the same way.

Mike, in his own understated way, had constantly nudged me to be faithful to church and to every Christian duty. He set the example for me to follow. Despite his popularity, his gifted abilities, and his many opportunities to revel in himself, I saw him only ever to be a humble, positive witness. He demonstrated the virtues of a dedicated follower of Christ to anyone who was watching. He truly embodied this verse from 1 Peter: "Be prepared to give an answer...for the hope that you have" (3:15).

One truth bonded us together forever—we went to heaven when we died, because we were prepared to go there. We had trusted Jesus with our destinies, and God rewarded us with an eternal home.

Mike's earthly pilgrimage was brief but highly influential, especially for me. He was so genuine and accepted me as a friend. I wanted to model the kind of consistent life Mike had—a truly authentic faith in Jesus Christ. And offer my life to others in the same way Mike offered his life to me.

Chapter 7

Charlie Dingman

Dr. Damon Vaughn was my pastor at First Baptist Church. When I felt God call me to the ministry, I told Pastor Vaughn and he was quick to encourage me. During my college years, he left First Baptist and went to another state. In 1984, Dr. Vaughn returned to Bossier City, but this time as pastor of Airline Baptist Church.

One day I received a phone call from him. "Would you consider serving on my staff at Airline Baptist as my assistant pastor?" he asked. He gave me a wonderful sales pitch.

It wasn't needed, because I would have followed him anyplace. "I feel deeply honored," I said.

For three years I made pastoral visits with him, helped him plan church events, conducted funerals and weddings alongside him, and preached in his absence. Most of all, I learned from that godly man.

During those three years, the growth of the Airline Church was explosive. Within months after I joined the staff, our church programs grew so rapidly we had to rent space on Sundays from

Greenacres Junior High School, located across the street. Still we grew, and rented the staterooms at the Rose-Neath Funeral Home next door for weekday Bible study classes. The Rose-Neath Funeral Home has had a significant role in the growth of the church. I didn't cause the growth, but I'm glad I was there and part of the excitement when it took place.

As the assistant pastor of Airline Baptist, I spent a lot of time doing administrative work in the church office. Since our church facility was located on a main thoroughfare, we experienced many transients stopping by for various needs. Some faced authentic financial crises; others were emergency family needs. And frankly, some were folks out to take advantage of benevolent ministries.

That's where Charlie Dingman really helped me. He'd been at Airline for decades. He remembered the days when someone would stop in for financial assistance and the church was almost as poor as the clients. Despite that, he exhibited an even hand when evaluating needs.

He possessed a kind of sixth sense about those with legitimate needs and those who were out to take what they could get. If anything, Charlie erred on the side of benevolence. After all, he was the chair of the benevolence committee. From that even-handed, compassionate, no-nonsense, wise Christian, I learned so much about helping the needy.

When souls have pressing needs, they don't need a Bible tract and someone to say, "We can't help, but God bless you." They need food or diapers or money for the rent or for the gas bill in winter. Or perhaps a place to sleep that night.

Charlie was excited that our church had finally become so blessed we were in a position to bless others. He prayed that that would happen and it did!

The return of Dr. Vaughn to Bossier and the massive growth that followed were halcyon days in the history of Airline Baptist Church. That's truly amazing, because only months before, the small congregation had considered closing its doors. Now, those doors were bursting open with phenomenal growth and meeting incredible needs.

That's important to know in what follows.

As assistant pastor, I was called on to help perform nearly every function that the senior pastor did. Among those many ministries was hospital visitation.

One day an urgent call came into the church office. Linda Thorn, one of our staff musicians, told us her father, Charlie Dingman, was in the intensive care unit. Within an hour I stood outside the ICU, ready to see Charlie.

In the ICU, I wondered if it would be our last time together. I knew Virginia and Charlie Dingman well and liked them. They had been one of the few remaining couples of the faithful remnant that had held on for years at Airline Baptist as the church dramatically declined. Charles W. Dingman, a retired salesperson for the Continental Bakery, also served as a school patrolman for the Greenacres Junior High School across the street from Airline Baptist. Charlie was elected a deacon by the church years earlier—a biblically ordained calling to serve and minister for the Lord.

A diminutive man, Charlie suffered from a host of ailments, any of which could have ended his life. I entered the room and said hello to him. The whir of life-sustaining machines continued during our conversation as I stood by his bed. Through his oxygen mask he smiled feebly.

I smiled back.

I leaned forward and took his hand. "Charlie, we gotta get you out of here," I said. "We need you back at Airline Baptist Church, where you belong." I indicated for him not to respond. "I want you to save your strength. I came by to check on you, to encourage you, and to let you know I care about you." I told him I wanted to pray for him before I left. He nodded.

Between wheezes and coughs, he thanked me for coming. Then he cleared his throat and said with great gravity, "I'm so glad God brought you . . . and your family here . . . to serve at Airline."

I nodded. "Seeing what God is doing here now is one of the most exciting things I've ever witnessed. You know, Charlie, my twin boys, Chris and Joe, just gave their hearts to Jesus and are going to be baptized."

Charlie's face beamed under the oxygen mask. But I sensed that he was about to share something that would be deep and unforgettable.

"There's something I have to tell you . . ." he said, pausing every few words to gain a breath. "Something I haven't told anyone before."

My heart raced. *Is this going to be one of those final, deathbed confessions?* I braced myself for a dramatic revelation.

"Do you remember . . . the last few Sundays when the church auditorium . . . has been packed to overflowing?"

I laughed. Asking a pastor if he remembers when his church auditorium has been packed to overflowing is like asking a barber if he likes heads full of shaggy hair. "Yes, Charlie, I remember the absolutely full church auditorium. It's been wonderful."

"Seeing that happen every week . . . has been one . . . of the greatest joys in my life." As Charlie continued, tears gently rolled down his timeworn face.

I waited, sensing he still hadn't really told me what was in his heart.

He stared into my eyes and said, "Years ago, I served on the building committee...voted to build the auditorium...where we currently worship...took some convincing to get the church family...to build it." He coughed and took several deep breaths. A tight smile appeared on his face. "Some folks laughed at us." Despite his weak condition, he tightened his grip on my hand and I felt the pressure of his fingers.

Continuing with the wheezing and coughing interruptions, he said, "Behind our backs...others said...we'd never fill the auditorium. After a while...I began to wonder...if they weren't right. Instead of the church growing...the congregation continued to shrink...Just a handful of souls left...rattling around in that big building each week...heartbreaking." He took several deep breaths.

"One Sunday...after a particularly pitiful attendance, I stayed inside, got on my knees in front of the altar, prayed, 'God, please let me live...long enough to see our church...filled...just once. If I could see that...I'd die a happy man.'"

I squeezed Charlie's hand in response. His smile was so big that it was visible even through his oxygen mask.

Laboriously he continued to speak, even though I tried to get him to conserve his strength. He shook his head. He needed to tell me, so I listened despite his frequent pauses.

"You might not know this, but I taught Sunday school in this church...since 1960...even when there was hardly anyone there to teach...but, oh, my brother...these past few months...have been some of the happiest of my life. That first Sunday...when the place was packed...I thought this old heart would explode.

It didn't…but it's just about worn out, anyway…I don't know how much longer I'm going to be here on earth…but I know that I can now die a happy man…I've lived long enough to see God…answer my deepest prayer." He paused again, grabbing for breath, and added, "Thank God."

Right there in the ICU, Charlie and I each offered prayers of thanksgiving to God for answering the prayers of many to see Airline Baptist Church filled to overflowing.

Charlie Dingman recovered from his experience in the ICU and lived a few more months of earthly life. He went to be with the Lord in January 1987, at the age of seventy-nine.

During his last days, he saw even greater church growth, a continued confirmation of Charlie's vision and dedicated commitment.

Today, Charlie would beam with joy, knowing that the building that he so courageously fought to construct is still serving Bossier City as a house of God. It's now a different congregation called Freedom Church. Airline Baptist Church grew so large that it relocated a few miles farther north on Airline Drive. Dr. Vaughn retired and became pastor emeritus.

Charlie's faith, vision, and work continue to serve the Lord long after his sweet soul went to be with Jesus.

After my car crash, when I went to be with the Lord, Charlie was standing there with the rest of the welcoming committee. His once-frail body was young and healthy—better than I had ever seen it on earth.

Charlie Dingman's inspiration and patience had a profound

impact on my life and ministry. His effective prayers and persever-
ance helped me make it through many difficult times of discour-
agement. Meeting a man here on earth whose legacy of vision,
faith, and prayers was rewarded against all odds encourages me to
this day. Every time I consider praying for the humanly impossible,
I think of Charlie. Praying, believing, and receiving are Charlie's
heritage.

I wish I could shout each week to the people who enter the
old home of Airline Baptist Church, "This is the place of worship
that Charlie prayed into being!" He lived long enough to see his
prayers answered. What a legacy! I continue to pray that we will
all live long enough to see our prayers answered. And that we will
be greeted at the gates by those who helped us get there.

Chapter 8

Sue Belle McRea Guyton

It wasn't just a happy accident in 1970 when the elevator door opened on the first floor of Graham Hall, a men's dormitory at Louisiana State University, and Darrell Guyton stood there. When he saw me, he smiled. Countless times I've thanked God for that moment. Both of our families were members of First Baptist Church of Bossier City. Darrell was from Airline High School, and I was a Bossier High kid, so we didn't have a lot of interaction except at church and on most weekends during the long, tedious five-hour drive back and forth to Bossier City from LSU in Baton Rouge. In those days, we had no interstate highway, and we drove the 250 miles in either his rattletrap or mine. Before we got cars, we carpooled with other Bossier City boys. Five college guys with their dirty laundry in a Ford Mustang was a lot of togetherness. Mostly we just slept on that exhausting trip in the early 1970s. If Darrell wasn't driving, he could nod off to sleep before we had even backed out of the driveway.

Darrell's dad, Marlyn Guyton, was on the staff of First Baptist Church. In those days, many churches had large bus ministries, where area-wide kids were picked up and brought to church. Darrell's dad was the head of that bus ministry, so of course I knew who his dad was. Darrell's mother, Sue Guyton, was an elementary school dietitian at Bellaire Elementary. Years after Darrell and I finished college, my daughter, Nicole, ate Mrs. Guyton's lunches at Bellaire as a kindergartner.

Darrell was a varsity basketball player at Airline High, so he played against my friend Mike Wood.

Tragically, Darrell's father was killed in a car crash on a fishing trip two days before Christmas 1970. We were stunned by the news of his death. Although I had already experienced loss, I was still young, and I didn't know what to say to the family.

That day on the elevator in the dorm I said, "It was such a shock about your dad." Not knowing what else to say, I added, "I know you guys were close. I'm sorry about his death."

"Thank you. Yeah, it was a shock." Then Darrell looked directly at me and said, "But we'll get through this. God has been good to us."

Then I asked him, "What floor are you on?"

"I'm on the fourth floor," Darrell said.

"I don't know how much longer I'm going to stay on the third floor," I said. "My roommate dropped out of school, so they're probably going to move me to another place."

"Really?" he said. "I'm going to need a roommate next semester because mine is moving to another dorm."

When we arrived at the third floor, I turned to say good-bye and he got off with me. We kept talking while he followed me to my half-empty dorm room, though it was already nine o'clock at night.

I can't tell you much about our conversation, but it seemed that one thing led to another. When the sun came up the next day, we were still talking. Somewhere during those hours together, we decided that we were going to be roommates. We were for two years, and we also became close-knit brothers for life.

Before that evening on the elevator, I used to see Darrell from my backyard because he dated Karen Lee, whose yard backed up to ours.

After Darrell and I became roommates, Karen introduced me to her good friend Eva Pentecost. They were both musicians, Karen an organist and Eva a pianist. They played in the Sunday night services at Barksdale Baptist Church, a smaller church in Bossier City.

On weekends when we drove the five hours from Baton Rouge to Bossier City, Darrell and I went to our home church in the morning, then on Sunday evenings we went to Barksdale Baptist, where he could see Karen.

On the other side of the platform from Karen, Eva Pentecost played the piano. That was the first time I really noticed her. Two years later, on December 30, 1972, Karen and Darrell were married at Barksdale. Eva and I were members of their wedding party.

One year later, almost to the day, Eva and I became husband and wife on December 29, 1973. Karen and Darrell were happy to return the favor and be a part of our wedding.

———◆———

Naturally, I got to know Darrell's family well. They were wonderful people, incredibly kind and welcoming. From the early days when I got to know the Guytons, Darrell's father, mother, brother, and two sisters all came out in the front yard every time we left for Baton Rouge. They hugged and kissed Darrell as if he were going away for five years. The rest of us boys in the college carpool didn't have that kind of incredibly close and affectionate family, and that made quite an impression on us.

I couldn't read the minds of the other guys who waited in the car for Darrell to finish the hugs and kisses, but I suspected their thoughts might have gone something like this: *Wow, would you look at that? My family never does that. These people really love each other and show it. They don't care who knows.* I surmise that at least a little envy might have even been felt. I know I had some.

Many times, I'd compare my own situation. When I was a little kid, my dad kissed me good night. He was career Army and went off to war far too often. He wrote me letters and signed them, "Love, Dad." After I left childhood, Dad no longer hugged or kissed me, and we never showed affection like I witnessed between six-foot-four-inch, two-hundred-pound Darrell and his barrel-chested, bald-headed, two-hundred-fifty-pound dad. However, late in his life my dad and I became increasingly affectionate. I cherish those memories.

My first college days were overwhelmingly difficult for me emotionally. All the positive affection and influence I had felt at church left me. I visited several churches in Baton Rouge, tried to become involved, but it didn't work. I lived alone in the dorm, so motivating myself to go to church alone wasn't always successful.

Besides that, being away at college was new for me. No one in my family had ever gone to college. There was no one to say, "Do this, don't do this, your priorities are out of order." I was on my own, and I wasn't coping well.

I began drinking and experimented with drugs. With my sheltered background and limited spiritual depth, I was especially lacking discipline and had little accountability.

That behavior changed after Darrell and I faced each other in the elevator. He became my close friend and my confidant—my moral rudder. Instead of condemning me or telling me I was doing something wrong, he'd ask, "Are you sure you should do that? Maybe you need to reconsider your decision." Or he might say, "Why don't we go do this instead?"

He constantly found wholesome things for us to do, and I'm more grateful than I could ever put into words. Not for one second have I doubted that God planted Darrell Guyton on the Graham Hall elevator that day.

After his father's death, Darrell, as firstborn, took on a lot of responsibility. He felt he needed to be the man of the house and help make decisions. Darrell didn't disappoint; he wore the mantle well. He continued mourning for his father, but mostly he kept it inside.

Darrell not only became my cheerleader and encourager, he became my best friend. He's still one of my closest friends. I could dial his number right now and he'd say, "When and where do you want to meet?"

As I look back, I realize we needed each other. Darrell had lost his dad, who was his best friend. He needed a confidant—someone who would listen to him. It was a privilege to be there to help wipe away his emotional tears, even if I seldom saw the wet ones. I learned to be a good listener, though I admit I listened mostly because I rarely knew what to say.

Darrell's mother, Sue Belle McRea Guyton, obviously loved her kids—deeply. And it was obvious everywhere, not only on the front lawn where they were kissing each other. No matter when I saw them, her four children were foremost in her mind. After Mr. Guyton was killed in the car crash, she was responsible for those kids, and Darrell was in college. I never figured out how they managed financially, but they did.

I enjoyed going to the Guyton house, and found excuses to hang around a lot. I told myself it was because Mrs. Guyton was such a fine cook—which was true. Food was her profession. She usually had something delicious cooking. But it was more than that. She loved me. I have no doubt about that.

At nineteen years of age, I was constantly hungry and went there to mooch. No matter how much I ate at home, I had room for whatever Sue Guyton offered.

"It sure smells good in here," was a common statement I made—and apparently the right one.

"Would you like some?"

Naturally, I hesitated in the early days and said, "Well, yes, ma'am, if there's enough. I don't want to—"

"Oh, no, we have plenty. Come on and sit down." And she always had enough.

Time after time I sat at her table, feasting on her tasty concoctions, but I also talked about things that troubled me.

And she listened. As I told her about what I was doing or had done, of course I left out the things that I shouldn't have done. Somehow, she knew—she had intuitive insight. But not once did I ever feel she looked down on me or judged me.

She was full of encouragement and wisdom, but she did it with laughter and warm kindness, telling me if I was doing something wrong, but in such a way that she never sounded judgmental or like she had all the answers. In her loving way, she pointed out right choices and directions for me, but she never made me feel like she was going to hassle me about them. Perhaps with the death of her beloved husband and surrounded by elementary kids all day, she enjoyed having a cup of coffee and talking with semi-adults like Darrell and his roommate, Don.

I had never known anyone before like Sue Belle Guyton. It was easy to see why Darrell became so charming and wise. He got that from her.

I used to say to some of my friends, "When you're loved by the Guytons, you're really loved. They know how to do it."

———◆———

One day I drove up to the house to pick up Darrell, but he had gone out and hadn't yet returned. Sue came to the door, and apologized for Darrell. "I just don't know where he is. He's not usually this late." That was true. He was a very punctual person.

"It's all right," I said. "We're not in any particular hurry; we'll get there." That also was true. And honestly, I had come a little early to see her and, yes, to see what was cooking.

"Come on in and have a seat," she said. "I've got brownies in the oven."

"Yes, ma'am, I can smell them. Thank you."

Within minutes, she put three or four brownies on a plate and I tried not to stuff them into my mouth at once.

As we chatted, she seemed different—not like her usual upbeat self. I hadn't seen her that way since the early days following Marlyn's death, and I had no idea what was going on. Back then,

I was a naïve twenty-year-old kid and didn't think about how difficult it must have been for her to raise four kids by herself. I knew it must have been tough, but I couldn't possibly understand.

She sat down across from me in her living room and slowly munched on her own brownie. Finally, she smiled at me and said, "I'm grateful God has brought you into Dee's life" (which was what she called Darrell and so did I after our friendship became close). "You've been a dear friend to him. I'm not sure how he would have coped at LSU without you."

"Yes, ma'am. Dee's a strong, smart young man. He'll do fine wherever life takes him. I couldn't have coped without him; Dee has become the best friend I've ever had."

Her eyes became misty and I thought she might burst into tears, but she didn't. "I'm sure you know that Darrell and his dad were close. Very close."

"Yes, ma'am, I do." Immediately my mind flashed back to the front lawn hug-and-kiss festival that frequently took place only a few feet from where we were currently eating brownies.

About that time, Dee burst through the door. "Uh, sorry I'm running late. I'll be with you in a couple of minutes." He rushed past to go into his room.

"Don't worry about it," I called out. "We'll get there when we get there. Besides, I've got some serious work to do on these brownies."

Once he was out of earshot, Mrs. Guyton said, "You know, Marlyn and Darrell loved each other very much."

"Yes, ma'am, Dee has talked about his dad often. He misses him deeply and I can only imagine how losing Mr. Guyton must really feel to all of you." As the words rolled off my tongue, I realized how hollow they must have sounded. It occurred to me that

I didn't know how those without Christ and the hope of everlasting life could ever function without knowing that their loved ones were safe in the arms of Jesus.

I was shaken out of my serious thoughts by her next words.

"Dee has a lot on his shoulders, you know, and I depend on him. Karen depends on him." He was then seriously considering asking her to marry him. She cleared her throat. "I just feel that they'll probably get married one day. His brothers and sisters look up to him. He changed his major in college, you know."

I nodded because I knew he had started LSU as an architecture major, which was a very, very difficult curriculum—five years of night and day building construction projects to get his bachelor's degree. He changed his major to education, which was a four-year course of study.

"I'm a little worried about him." She looked down at her hands. "I know he has to have been devastated by his dad's sudden death. They were such buddies. You and Dee are both growing into such fine young men."

I smiled at her, aware that she had something she still wanted to say.

She stared at me. "I've hardly seen Dee express his emotions following his dad's death. You know, he just can't keep that bottled up inside him. It'll eat him up."

"Yes, ma'am."

She put her hand on mine. "You don't have to answer this if you don't feel comfortable with it. And I'm not asking you to give away any secrets, or betray any trusts, but does Dee ever express any feelings or emotions that you have seen following his dad's death?"

Even while she formed her question, I was reflecting on the times after a call from home that Dee became emotional. I tried to leave our room to give him privacy but sometimes I couldn't get away fast enough. That's when he sometimes broke down and talked about the painful turns his life had taken. I can't say I was particularly well equipped to help him, but I was there to listen, to encourage, to give him space if he needed it, to just leave him alone for a while, or just to give him a big hug, which probably should have been more comfortable than it was.

My heart went out to him on those days after we returned from a weekend in Bossier or he received a call from Sue or Karen. Sometimes after the lights were off in our dorm room, I sensed from the other side of the room that the tears were slipping slowly down his face.

Mrs. Guyton's soft words shook me from my thoughts and my brownie.

"You don't have to say anything. Just nod if you feel like he's working his way through this emotionally. Just nod," she said with great gravity, more than I'd ever heard her speak before.

She'd hardly finished before she began to weep gently. It seemed like an amalgam of smiles and tears at the same time. She had to know that at any moment Dee would barge into the room and see her mixed emotions. (Dee always barged into a room.)

I wasn't torn between keeping Dee's privacy versus giving his mother peace of mind. To me there never was a question. I felt caught up in how amazingly complicated life can be. Here was a mother's love for her son on full display; in private, I witnessed a son's love for his father. Both poignant and completely sincere. She needed to know from someone who knew and loved Dee and would keep his confidence. I believed she needed to know that, in his own way, he was working through his father's death and trying to be the man that his father would want him to be.

I looked into Sue Guyton's sweet eyes and nodded. That was my way of saying, "Yes, your son is expressing his deeply held emotion about the death of Marlyn as best he can." And I believe she knew that if I felt he needed her or anyone else to help him during those trying times, we'd be there for him.

She smiled, even though I didn't say a word. "That's all I need you to say." Hurriedly, she dried her tears. And she shared with me one of the wisest truths I have ever heard. "My Marlyn was the strongest man I've ever known. Physically and every other way. He was strong enough to tear a phone book in half, but he had an inner power that I found very strong and appealing. Many times, he wept over his bus-ministry kids whose parents made them stop riding the church bus. I'd witness his weeping because parents deprived their kids of a chance to hear about Jesus. I'd seen him weep over his own children as he talked about how much he loved them and how much he loved me. He wasn't ever afraid to let me know how he felt. How blessed he was."

Not knowing how to respond, I nodded again.

"I look back on it now, Don, and I thank God for giving me such a strong and caring man. I always knew how deeply he felt about everything. And I always thought of my husband's tears as strong man's tears."

She clutched my hand. "Don't ever be afraid to express how you feel about things. Don't keep the important stuff buried inside. Tears show how deeply you feel about something. Don't be afraid."

I'm not sure how I responded. I remember thinking that she believed that her husband was a strong and godly man. And he was. And I distinctly remember thinking: *This is a strong and godly woman.*

With her handkerchief in her lap and her hands now clasped, she said softly, "Thank you for being a good friend to my son."

I was savvy enough to know that I had been part of a teachable moment and that I had been gifted with a great truth. Many times after that, I'd receive great truths from Sue Guyton. It still amazed me that she continued to offer me counsel after a cruel loss or a hurtful disappointment—she never failed to reach out to me.

For years I struggled with my emotions about many things. At the worst of times, I'd think back to the Guyton living room with brownies on a plate on the coffee table and the smiling face of Mother Guyton and her awesome counsel.

"If my Jesus wept at the tomb of His friend Lazarus," she said, "then it's okay for you and for Dee to weep strong men's tears."

Just then Dee's door opened, and he yelled, "I'm finally coming!"

That was the end of that conversation, but not the last time she spoke wise words to me. Many, many times I opened up to her because I knew she wouldn't laugh and she'd answer me truthfully.

For instance, I fell in love with Eva and knew I wanted to marry her. Sue Belle was one of the first friends I shared the news with. "I want to know what it's like to be married. How do we stay together and make the most of our lives?"

Again, she didn't fail me. Most of her guidance wasn't complicated. Sound, practical advice. Whether life decisions about my calling or when we became parents, she rejoiced and was supportive.

Once I asked her about how to get past disagreements in marriage. I meant fights, because Eva and I were having one. She smiled and said, "Don't worry too much about that, because if you don't have fights, then you must not love each other very much."

I must have looked puzzled, because the way things were going and according to the Guyton School of Theology, Eva and I loved each other a lot!

"It's not the arguments; it's how you go about solving them. At your wedding, the preacher said, 'What God has joined together, let no man put asunder.' That means that both of you have a solemn obligation to work things out.

"If God is the glue that binds you together—and He is—even if you're not getting along, you're still bound to her by your mutual faith in God. He completes that triangle."

"But you and Mr. Guyton—you didn't ever have any arguments, did you?"

She threw her head back and laughed. "You're not serious, are you? Sure, we disagreed. We tried to keep our disagreements away from the kids, especially when they were young." She paused before she added, "When you argue, and you will, fight fair. Don't bring up failures or past mistakes. Focus on the things you can fix and then fix them. By all means, understand that there are some things you aren't going to agree on. If you have to agree to disagree, do it and move on. I mean that. Don't circle the runway and come back to that. If you do, you haven't agreed to disagree; you've disagreed to agree to disagree."

As if she were checking off things not to do, I was checking boxes inside my head. I kept thinking, *I'm not rating very well on this fight thing.* And I wasn't.

Probably the best counsel I received was specific to Eva and me. In those days, Eva was what we'll call high-strung (she had a temper and couldn't understand why I didn't). She mistook my not yelling or throwing things as not caring. I preferred to talk it out. She took that as a lack of interest.

On that point she might have been partially correct. I had to learn to become more engaged, more responsive, even if it meant raising my voice. She had to understand that her irritability and anger didn't move me. It just turned me off.

That's what Sue meant by communicate clearly and fight fairly. When Eva and I began to grow in that, we made headway and solved differences. We even sometimes agreed to disagree.

"The very best thing about having a fight," she chuckled and said, "is making up."

After Darrell and Karen had married, I told everyone who knew us, "He swapped me for a better roommate."

"Certainly a prettier one," someone said.

After graduating from LSU and working in the broadcasting business for a few years, I answered a call to ministry and went to seminary in New Orleans. I didn't see much of Darrell or the Guyton family.

In the ensuing years, Sue Guyton wasn't ever far from my mind. She had an inner depth of faith that had a profound effect on me. No matter what happened, she never wavered. Her husband had died, and she was left with providing for four kids on a dietitian's salary. Not once did I hear her utter the words "Poor me," or anything that hinted at self-pity. In a way that was beyond my maturity, she was able to see God's loving hand in everything that happened. Always committed to helping others, Sue was responsible for helping found a single adult ministry at First Baptist Bossier.

Life was challenging for her, and she wasn't afraid to talk about her problems. One time she told me, "I'm really struggling, Don, but God's peace fills my heart. Every day, I pray for my children and for you. I'm here for you."

What did she see in me? I don't know, but I think it was my neediness—my craving for emotional guidance and support combined with my openness to learn. And no matter what my circumstances (and I opened my heart to her), her answer always came in practical ways with the reminder that Jesus loved me as He loved her and her family. Her words were so earnest, I never doubted her.

In March 1982, a phone call came from Karen. "It's Momma Guyton," she said.

Slowly the story unfolded. At age fifty-five, Sue Belle McRea Guyton lay in a coma in the Bossier City Medical Center not ten blocks away from her front yard on Lincoln Street, where that hugging and kissing had taken place. She had contracted viral encephalitis at school.

Brokenhearted, as if I was losing my own mother, I prayed for Karen and Darrell and the other Guytons. Although the prognosis was negative, we asked God to spare the life of that godly woman if it was His will.

Four days past her fifty-fifth birthday, Sue Guyton went to be with the Lord. No doubt, she was greeted at the gates by big, strong Marlyn. I know from my own experience that there were no tears there, only glorious bliss.

At her memorial service, I couldn't help shedding some tears. Of all the people I've ever known, she would understand where those tears came from. She was certainly among the most courageous, faithful, and wise individuals I've ever had the pleasure of meeting here on earth.

On the day I died, Sue Belle Guyton was alongside the other greeters at the gate. She smiled sweetly, embraced me, and was at my side as we walked toward the gate. That day at the gates, there were hugs and kisses on "God's front porch." And when I entered heaven, Sue had arms reaching out to embrace me. She wasn't wearing her starched white dietitian uniform with matching white shoes—the way she was usually dressed when I visited the house. Like everyone else, Sue wore a white robe.

More than anyone else I'd met at that stage of my life, Sue made it clear that Jesus was the one who was taking her through her loss and loneliness. If there were doubts, I never sensed them.

Sue Belle Guyton taught me so much about life.

Sue was such an astute, compassionate woman. Many, many times at their home, her wise counsel flowed.

Although she wasn't instrumental in my coming to know Jesus Christ, her loving counsel kept me moving forward on earth, so I could meet her one day in heaven.

Sue Belle exhibited God's compassion to me and made me glad not only that I knew Jesus Christ, but also that I had a role model to follow. And that I have an absolute obligation to be one.

Chapter 9

Grandma Nellie Piper

When I entered the gates of heaven, one of the very first people I saw was one of the dearest to my heart: Grandma Nellie Piper. She was my grandmother and so much more.

I didn't realize it as a child, but Grandma Piper worked quietly to prepare me to follow Jesus. Although our family wasn't churched, she clearly demonstrated for us that some of God's best influences didn't always take place inside a church building. She loved me to Jesus. Whenever I reflect on Grandma Piper, I think of the times I stared into her soft brown eyes. At that age, I couldn't have put my emotions into words, but in her I saw Jesus.

Nellie Clemens married Edgar Piper and left her family's farm in Western Illinois where she had been born. They migrated to Southeast Arkansas to settle in the Mississippi delta town of Monticello.

Grandpa Edgar Piper went to be with the Lord in 1948, two years before I was born. For the next fourteen years, Nellie Piper was a widow with ten children. Her youngest son, Ralph, was my father. He left Arkansas in 1943 to fight Hitler and he never came back to live in his native state. Although he met my mother, Billie Kulbeth, while she was still at Drew Central High School in Monticello, they didn't marry until 1949.

Following their wedding, Dad's career in the US Army took them overseas to France, Germany, and back to the United States to Massachusetts. We moved from there to Florida, Texas, and Louisiana. But no matter where we lived in the States, we made at least two annual pilgrimages to Monticello. My dad had nine brothers and sisters, and my mom had only one sister. On those visits to Monticello, we visited my grandmother, great-grandparents, and an assortment of second, third, and kissing cousins.

Nellie Piper lived in a two-bedroom white clapboard house with green trim on North Rose Street in Monticello, Arkansas. That short street ran at a ninety-degree angle to Godbold Street, where my mother's grandparents Hattie and J. R. Mann lived. Those two streets were kept from intersecting by railroad tracks, situated at an angle between them. No vehicular traffic could pass from one street to the other, only foot traffic. I could see both my grandparents' houses, Piper and Mann, from their front yards. To this day, I haven't decided who lived on the wrong side of the tracks. I think that neither family did; both were poor in material things but rich in love.

During each visit to Monticello, what I most remember is the distinctive, dignified, and lonely figure of Nellie Piper, always dressed in flowered gingham housedresses with her hair pulled up into a tightly wound bun.

Grandma Nellie survived enormously trying times after her husband died. Yet she exhibited great strength, dignity, and serenity in the midst of poverty and loneliness in her little clapboard house on North Rose. Her brown eyes disclosed a kindness and a wisdom that

I seldom ever encountered in others. Later in my life, I reflected that she lived the apostle Paul's words to the church at Philippi: "For I have learned to be content whatever the circumstances" (Philippians 4:11). Many times, over the years, when I've read that verse, my mind has gone immediately to Grandma. She *lived* that verse. She loved to tell me, "I do my best and trust God for the rest."

When we stayed at her house, some nights when I awakened, I'd get out of bed and see Grandma sitting at her kitchen table, a single incandescent bulb hanging from a single strand, lighting her Bible. With glasses on the tip of her nose, Benjamin Franklin style, she was poring over God's Word. Fascinated by that sight, I often stood noiselessly and watched her turning the now-fragile and well-marked pages. Her face beamed with utter rapture, as if she had received a special word from on high.

While I lingered, after a time, Grandma would solemnly close her Bible in such a way that it seemed to me she was reluctant to stop reading. Then she'd push her Bible to the other side of the table, bow her head, and clasp her hands together on the table. And she'd start talking to God.

I could rarely hear the words, but I didn't need to. The softness of her voice impressed me that it was as if she was talking to someone she loved. Even today, when I think of my grandmother, I can see her praying. As I silently observed her, I sensed that prayer was more than a duty. For her, it was a way of life.

My grandmother modeled two great gifts from God for me—reading her Bible and praying quietly. I don't think she ever realized I watched her on those cold winter nights. But to me, it was transformative to see my grandma Piper, living in near poverty, and in solitude, seeking God's guidance in prayer and study.

If I close my eyes now, I can still see her in the glow of the single light, Bible in front of her, hands clasped, completely focused on the God who sustained her.

Thank you, Grandma.

We made other trips to Monticello, but twice a year our family was certain to be there at Christmastime and family reunions. For the first few years of my life, I marveled that Santa Claus was able to find us no matter where we were on Christmas Eve.

Grandma Piper's house was so small, we were usually the only ones staying there with her. Grandma kept a parakeet in her parlor that she adored.

One of the special things about visiting Grandma Piper was listening to her parakeet singing all the time. It struck me even then as a child that always having something to sing about was remarkable. That little parakeet gave her pleasure. With her hard life, she needed that joy.

Being a country boy at heart, I was accustomed to all manner of feathered creatures. We had geese, guineas, chickens, and pheasants while growing up. But Grandma Piper's bird was completely different. I often wondered how so much sound could come out of such a small bird. That parakeet awakened us early on Christmas morn. The little bird seemed to sing with even greater intensity and joy at Christmastime.

When my brothers and I joyfully and anxiously opened our presents, I learned quite young what to expect from Grandma Piper. Each year, it was the same gift—three white handkerchiefs neatly sealed in cellophane. Many Christmases passed before I realized what a sacrifice that must have been for her to purchase even that humble gift for dozens of grandchildren. I now understand that the sacrifice was part of the gift.

The other annual trip to Monticello was for Piper family reunions. At first, they were held in Grandma's backyard. As the family grew, we moved the activities to the city park. Each time, following a prayer, a plethora of Pipers descended on tables laden with casseroles, chicken prepared in every conceivable manner, fresh farm-grown vegetables, glorious desserts, and sweet tea, always sweet tea. Too many adults claimed the chairs, so we kids sat around on blankets on the ground.

After the feast, the men gravitated together and swapped stories. The women congregated and chatted, especially the do-you-remember-when banters. Inevitably these memories included family members missing from the reunion, some infirm and some who had died.

Although I didn't sit near them, I observed their behavior and listened to their laughter. I could tell when they discussed sad stories, especially the death of someone they loved. Their voices grew softer, and serious looks covered their faces.

After the remembrances of lost loved ones, often the mood lightened as aunts and uncles spoke of happier times and the often-hilarious deeds of our deceased family members.

Gaggles of kids ran around, tumbled, squealed, and played ring around the rosie, red rover, statue of liberty, and marbles. As dusk fell, Pipers picked up empty dishes, blankets, and stray kids, and wearily loaded their cars and trucks. Much hugging and kissing ensued, which from us kids dissolved into sleepy waves. So long for another year in the Piper chronicles.

Those wonderful gatherings of Pipers were enjoyable until the year Grandma Piper became the subject of those missing from

the reunion. Our beloved grandmother Nellie Piper had long suffered from heart problems as well as diabetes. Ultimately, a stroke
claimed her life at the age of seventy-three in 1962.

Before she died, word reached us in Louisiana, where we were
stationed, that Grandma had been rushed to the Monticello hospital. My dad had just departed for a tour of duty in Korea, and the
Red Cross notified him aboard his troop ship that his mother was
seriously ill.

My mother, my three brothers, and I drove to Monticello and
held vigil outside her hospital room. Grandma seemed to rally
somewhat, so we returned to Louisiana to await hopeful news.

Only a few days later, a phone call pierced the night at our home
in Fort Polk, Louisiana. The matriarch of the Piper clan had gone
to be with the Lord.

As a twelve-year-old, I tried to lift the spirits of my mom and my
brothers. My youngest brother, Steve, was only two and had little comprehension of that momentous event. Mother, my middle
brother, Alan, and I began to gather our meager dress clothing and
prepared for the sad return to Monticello, and to my first funeral.
Papa and Grandma Kulbeth went with us. When my brothers and
I arrived in Arkansas, for our first-ever funeral, nothing could prepare us for what we were about to see. The trip with Mom to
Monticello was a quiet one. No doubt everyone was lost in their
own thoughts of Grandma Piper. Although I was twelve years old,
I had never lost a loved one.

Imagine my shock when we walked into Grandma's tiny house
on North Rose Street to acknowledge her death, and there she was
majestically laid out in the parlor, a common practice back then.
I'd never seen the body of a deceased person, much less my own
grandmother resting in a casket in her own house.

That first encounter with death traumatized me. Shock and horror filled my soul. Aunts hovered over the casket and, peering inside, said things such as, "Look, she's only sleeping." Or, "Doesn't she look real? They did a good job on her, didn't they?"

I was young and impressionable, but I still knew that the only honest response to those comments was, "No, no, she doesn't look real. No, they didn't do a good job on her. And no, she's not sleeping." But respectfully, I kept my thoughts to myself, reminding myself never to say those things.

Just then, I was diverted from my sad emotions by the parakeet. The bird was warbling ever so sweetly. The creature seemed entirely oblivious that a new owner was about to take over its care.

At that very moment, for Nellie Clemens Piper, the somber little bird had been superseded by the chorus of heavenly hosts. The flapping of a parakeet's wing was replaced by the holy beat of the wings of angels. The Piper family reunion in Monticello was a pale imitation of the one Grandma must have experienced when she arrived at the gates of heaven.

I can only imagine what it must have been like when his commanding officer summoned Dad to a cabin on the military transport ship in the middle of the Pacific Ocean to tell him his mother had died.

I know he was given the opportunity to be airlifted off the ship and flown stateside to attend her service. But that effort would have delayed Grandma Piper's funeral service for several days. Dad opted not to do so, knowing that the other family members would be waiting and mourning even longer. It would also have meant that his tour of duty in Korea would be extended for some time.

Months later when Dad returned from deployment in Korea, our family made the somber return to Green Hill Cemetery outside Monticello. Not once did I ever hear Dad speak about his mother's death. There Grandma Piper had been laid to rest beside Grandpa Edgar. Mom, Alan, Steve, and I watched quietly as Nellie's youngest son knelt to honor his mom and dad. It wasn't the reunion that he had hoped for. But praise God, forty years later, mother and son would see each other at the gates of heaven.

In her parlor on North Rose Street, all I saw in that casket the day of the funeral was the shell of Grandma Piper. She died on earth when I was twelve years old. When I was thirty-eight, I saw her again in heaven. At the gates of glory, my grandmother walked toward me in a shimmering resplendent robe, a far cry from the time I saw her in her casket. Her life demonstrated an unwavering faith in the face of terrifying odds. When I looked into Grandma's eyes there, I saw the indescribable joy of being home. Beaming ear to ear with a glorious smile—there's that smile again—and outstretched arms, welcoming me to our forever home. I had arrived because she had helped me get there.

She looked happier and more vibrant than at any time that I'd seen her in my childhood. Her hair wasn't in a bun. Only at night on North Rise Street had she taken out the bobby pins and let us see her beautiful long hair. Never once in the daylight. Seeing it long and flowing stunned me. She seemed younger, too, and yet as different as she was, I *knew* her.

In life, she seemed to have so much responsibility on her shoulders and wearied by it all—but she didn't complain. Now she was different. Her face shone with joy—even now those statements sound inadequate. Every facial muscle was relaxed and yet she glowed with a kind of ecstasy. Back on earth, many of her children and grandchildren had taken advantage of her and she worried about them. In heaven, all those burdens were gone, totally washed away. Outside Monticello, Arkansas, on County Road 15 is Green Hill Cemetery. Resting in the shade of the old oak trees are the earthly remains of Edgar and Nellie Piper. Etched on their grave marker are these words: "GONE HOME TO HEAVEN."

The words are exactly right.

Chapter 10

Joe Socks

Sitting in the back row of Grandma Piper's memorial service, I watched tears cascade down my grandfather's time-weathered cheeks. I'd never seen him cry before. My grandfather Joe Kulbeth, whom I called Papa, usually kept his sad feelings to himself. With no conscious effort on my part, I began to cry with him. Monticello, Arkansas, was such a small pastoral town in the 1940s when my parents met that everyone knew each other. Indeed my grandpa Joe Kulbeth and grandma Nellie Piper had known each other before my parents even met. And remember they lived across the tracks from each other as well. Since it was my first funeral it was still startling to see him crying for any reason. By this time, of course, Nellie was the mother-in-law of his daughter Billie.

After the service at Greenhill United Methodist Church, Papa and I went to a graveside service up the hill to the Piper family plot.

Like others of his generation, Papa had endured wretched poverty, survived the Great Depression, built ships for the Navy in

World War II, and through "blood, toil, and sweat," had achieved a measure of respectability. On the afternoon of Grandma Piper's funeral, his twelve-year-old grandson Donnie thought he was about the "swellest" person I'd ever known.

I still do.

I became the only family member with a college degree and he was proud of me. Even with my education, I considered him to be one of the smartest people I ever knew. I still feel that way. Many times, I saw my carpenter grandfather take piles of building materials and turn them into amazing structures. His handiwork dazzled me. I wanted to grow up to be like him.

I still do.

During the Great Depression, Papa Joe Kulbeth owned only one shirt and one pair of socks with holes in them. Each night, Grandmother Bonnie washed and dried those socks by a potbelly stove, so he could wear them to work the next day, where he earned one dollar a day.

Every day at noon, the lumberjacks ate their cold biscuits, sorghum syrup, and cured ham lunches. Before eating, they took off their work boots to give their tired feet a break. Seeing Joe's same holey socks each day, his coworkers teasingly nicknamed him Joe Socks. The nickname followed him to his grave.

Because my dad was so often away due to US Army obligations, Papa became more than a grandfather to me. In 1949, the year before I was born, Joe and Bonnie moved from Arkansas to Bossier City and made it their permanent home. Whenever my dad was transferred to a place where his dependents couldn't go, Mother and her boys moved back to Bossier.

Joe Socks became a union carpenter. I never knew him as anything but a builder—of buildings, bridges, highways, and subsequently, of men. As a maturing boy, I followed him like a puppy. I also noticed the many scars he bore on his body from grueling, often dangerous work.

He was even missing parts of five fingers: two on one hand and three on the other. But you better believe he never let those missing digits interfere with his labor!

Eventually, I was big enough to carry building materials for him, hand him equipment, and generally try to make myself useful. He was my consummate encourager. I must have been a nuisance sometimes and made mistakes with the wrong tools or the wrong nails, but he never let me know it.

As I grew older, I observed deeper aspects of Papa's life and learned that he couldn't read or write. I'd often wondered why he had me sign for all building materials and endorse his checks.

Like many others born before the Great Depression, Joe Kulbeth had dropped out of school to work so he and his family could eat. Papa covered his illiteracy so well that I was stunned by how well he functioned and how much he had accomplished.

Papa was hardly a saint, but I knew he loved and followed Jesus. He was a rough-hewn man's man, born during the most challenging times of the twentieth century. Joe Socks could be tough, but he was fair. He didn't go to church, and after I learned he was illiterate, I understood. He was afraid he'd be asked to pray or read the Bible aloud. Besides that, he once said he didn't have the proper clothes for church as his primary wardrobe consisted of overalls.

Many times, I watched my grandma and my mother getting dressed for church, wearing hats and gloves and high-heeled shoes. Papa would tell us good-bye when we left for worship and add, "Say a prayer for me."

We would have loved it if he'd gone with us. I believe he never felt worthy of his salvation or being in the presence of the redeemed. Despite that, love for God filled his heart. He had absorbed a lot of Scripture during his life. He'd often begin a sentence with, "The Good Lord says..." Then he'd give a down-home version of a great theological truth. He was so humbled that Jesus had been a builder, too. His words were often mangled, but I always got the drift of what he meant. Later as a pastor, I learned that sometimes those are the best words of all.

———◆———

Some of my biggest thrills in ministry were when Joe Socks sneaked into services when I preached in local churches. I'd spot his shock of white hair, fair complexion, and generous nose as he settled into the back pew. He was proud of me, but I have to say, I was proud of him.

Although Papa seldom expressed any kind of Christian experience like others I met in heaven, it was there—on the inside, where not everyone could see it. If they had observed his extraordinary kindnesses to others, his faithfulness, and his humility, they would have known that Jesus was in him and with him.

By seeing that quiet, unspoken commitment in Papa, I also learned to see and appreciate many followers of Jesus who serve quietly and with conviction as they go about their daily lives. Some people show their faith far better than they can talk about it. St. Francis of Assisi put it so well: "Preach the Gospel always, and if necessary, use words!" That was Papa.

———◆———

In 1981, I was in my eighth year as an executive at KSLA-TV, the CBS affiliate in the Shreveport-Texarkana market. Eva was expecting our twin boys. Our daughter, Nicole, the apple of Joe Socks's eye, was five years old. One night shortly after I'd arrived home from a long day at the station, the phone rang.

My frantic mother cried, "Come quick; Daddy's dying!"

Shocked by the prospect of losing Papa, I ran back to my just-parked car and raced out to my grandparents' home. As I entered the house, I was startled to see my dad performing CPR on his father-in-law. Just then, an ambulance pulled up and EMTs took over.

My mother and my grandmother, still in their nightclothes, were quietly weeping on each other's shoulders.

My dad, always a take-charge kind of guy, told me, "Ride in the ambulance with Papa to the hospital." He stayed with my mother and grandmother.

The scene was horrifying, and riding with an unconscious Papa in an ambulance to the hospital was even more so. With flashers on and sirens blaring, the driver reached the Bossier City Medical Center quickly. On a gurney, they rushed Papa into the ER. They wouldn't let me follow. Instead, they told me to fill out paperwork and then wait in the waiting room.

Within minutes, our family doctor, E. B. Robinson, emerged from Papa's room to inform us that Joe Socks had succumbed to "most likely a massive cardiac arrest." The doctor seemed heartbroken to announce the death of his good friend of many years.

Hardly aware of what I was doing, I began comforting the doctor. Suddenly I realized that Grandma, Mom, and Dad didn't know what was happening. I walked slowly to the pay phone in the waiting room and called Joe Socks's home.

"Joe Socks is gone," I said quietly.

The tools of this carpenter were silenced, and my heart was broken. I have suffered from a lot of broken bones in my body, but nothing hurts like a broken heart.

The ensuing days gave us an opportunity to grieve and celebrate the life of a country carpenter who had built the homes some of the mourners lived in. Joe Kulbeth built bridges on the highway in front of the cemetery where he is buried.

He'd exceeded the biblically proscribed seventy years mentioned in Psalm 90:10. Still, we wanted more earth time for Papa. Knowing the hard and demanding life that he'd lived, I realized Papa was so tired that one night he simply breathed his last breath and went home.

Through all the grieving, one thought brought me great peace—I knew Papa was in heaven, where he belonged. I sincerely believe that even though we might be surprised by who is in heaven, they're not!

As I shed tears at Joe Socks's gravesite, I vividly recalled the day when I saw him cry. In my mind, I can still see the tears that he shed at another memorial service twenty years earlier.

—————

Although both my parents had trusted Jesus as Lord at a young age, church attendance had not been a priority in their young adulthood. But from Papa we learned that when we'd done something wrong, we needed to acknowledge our failure and admit we needed forgiveness. We also knew that we had to do better the next time.

Papa tolerated no disrespect for Jesus. He was God-fearing and

God-affirming, a sinner saved by grace; and he defended those who tried to live holy lives.

Papa lived by two significant Scriptures: "Whatever you do, do it all for the glory of God" (1 Corinthians 10:31), and "Whatever your hands find to do, do it with all your might" (Ecclesiastes 9:10). Papa paraphrased it well: "You have to give a man an honest day's work for an honest day's wage."

———

Papa was the first person I saw when I arrived at the gates of heaven. Facing him was like hearing God say to me, "You were with him when he left earth; now he is here to greet your arrival from earth." Papa, more than any other person in my life, set the standard for following the Savior and for doing our earthly work well.

When I stared at Papa's face, I knew where I was, because I knew where he was. He had gone home to be with the Lord, and I had joined him.

"Welcome home, Donnie," he said.

I grinned when I heard that. After my childhood, only my grandparents called me by that name. I hadn't been called Donnie in many years.

As Papa reached out to embrace me, I stared at his hands. To my surprise, those missing fingers on each hand had been fully restored. On earth I had never seen complete hands on Papa. As he embraced his oldest grandson in heaven, I saw and felt them. He was perfect—just the way the Lord intended for us all.

One thing is certain: Never again will I see Papa cry.

There are no tears in heaven—only continuous joy, unspeakable bliss, and unending love with those who love us and with other saints we haven't even met yet. In heaven, there are no good-byes; only hellos.

When I return, I'll see Joe Socks again.

Chapter 11

J. R. and Hattie Mann

When I close my eyes, I can see an indelible image of my great-grandparents J. R. and Hattie Mann. They're standing on the edge of their whitewashed front porch on Godbold Street in Monti-cello, Arkansas. Grandpa Mann has his arm on Grandma's stooped shoulder. Their right hands are raised in a gentle wave.

An old, brown, shingle-sided house droops behind them. Grandpa is dressed in his starched khaki pants, suspenders, and a plaid shirt. His cotton-white hair is smartly combed and groomed with Brylcreem. Grandma is wearing her usual starched gingham dress, a plain white apron around her waist, and her tightly curled hair is still more black than gray. Bright sunshine glints from their gold-toned bifocals.

Grandpa James Robert Mann was of stern German stock. He was sometimes a tomato farmer, a Monticello town marshal, and a Bap-tist deacon. I can still envision the pearl-handled revolver he kept in a holster beside their feather bed. He wasn't to be trifled with. Yet he was incredibly tenderhearted and spent much of his time helping children at Monticello's Arkansas Baptist Children's Home.

As the oldest of his great-grandchildren, I adored him. My mother, Billie, was his oldest grandkid and I was her oldest. We often thought he bestowed his favor especially on us. He certainly was kind to me, and even though he didn't say the words, I never doubted that he loved me.

Grandpa Mann owned a rattletrap flatbed truck in which he hauled his tomatoes to market. When his grandkids gathered at the Mann house, he herded us onto the back of that truck and paraded us down Godbold Street. What a great adventure!

Grandma Mann was horrified that we enjoyed riding with Grandpa, especially because the bed of the truck didn't have any sides or railings. Later, we understood: Grandpa was one of the worst drivers in town. We never worried about his driving. For us, it was an adventure.

We knew Grandma loved us and worried about Grandpa's driving, especially when we were with him. Grandma was one of the most genuinely kind persons I've ever known. Soft-spoken with a charming sense of humor, she evoked admiration and joy from those around her. Although she was severely stooped by years of osteoporosis, Grandma Mann pressed on with only the slightest hint of her limitations. She didn't complain about pain or inconvenience with her condition. Complaining wasn't in her nature.

One of her defining features was her absence of teeth. Like many of her generation, including Grandpa, she lost her teeth at an early age. Grandpa was seldom without his dentures; Grandma rarely wore hers. The only times that I saw her wear her "store-bought" teeth were on Sundays when she went to church. Otherwise, the false teeth resided in a glass of water beside the sink in her kitchen, always "smiling" at us.

We adored Grandma and Grandpa Mann. It wouldn't have been

possible to have more admirable role models. They were faithful to each other for more than sixty years, faithful to their church, faithful to their family, and faithful to God.

One of my most treasured possessions is the large red Mann family Bible. Its spine is tattered from years of use. Many fingers of the Mann clan, including mine, have turned the yellowing pages. Typical of that kind of Bible, there is a genealogy section in which are written the births and deaths of our family's generations.

I consider it a sacred honor to be among those listed as progenies on its pages. Even more, what a privilege to have such devoted forebears as Grandpa and Grandma Mann.

In 1969, when I was a college student, Grandma Mann suffered a stroke and died a few days later at the age of seventy-five. Since that day, the light never seemed as bright on Godbold Street. Though he was devastated, Grandpa didn't display outward emotion to our family after her passing.

Despite efforts to involve him in other family activities or opportunities to travel, he soon began to languish, and then withdraw. A stroke brought him to the same hospital where Grandma Piper and Grandma Mann had died. Astonishingly, J. R. Mann was hospitalized for the first time in his eighty-two years of life.

Slightly more than a year after Grandma died, Grandpa Mann joined his lifelong sweetheart in heaven.

When the big truck hit me, I, too, approached this awesome celestial boulevard and that brilliant pearl entrance. And there to meet me were my two precious great-grandparents J. R. and Hattie Mann. My last earthly memory of them was when they stood, old and frail, and waved gently to me from their earthly porch in Arkansas.

In heaven, they were radiant, healthy, and strong.

Grandpa's pained expression following the loss of his precious wife was now replaced by an ecstatic smile of reunion. He glowed with peace and satisfaction. Grandma, once bowed with severe bone disease, now stood upright, unwrinkled, and un-aged, six inches taller in heaven.

She also had sparkling white teeth—her own! Nothing about her surprised and delighted me as much as seeing those beautiful teeth.

When I arrived at the gates of heaven, their faces beamed. It was the first time I'd ever seen their real smiles. The emotion behind their heavenly joy bespoke their enormous happiness and contentment. The perfection of their bodies announced complete physical healing and absolute wholeness.

J. R. and Hattie have changed addresses from Godbold Street in Monticello to God's golden street. In heaven, they've moved to a new and better front porch than the old, time-worn one on Godbold Street. And they were there, welcoming me home to God's front porch. They certainly helped me get there, too.

Chapter 12

Charlotte Jaynes

She was a slender wisp of a woman with a smile a mile wide. Charlotte B. Jaynes possessed a sassy sense of humor; however, in her classroom, she was strictly business. With a reputation for being a stern disciplinarian, she was also known for her fairness.

Miss Jaynes didn't work to produce equal results from her students, but she expected their best efforts in her classroom regardless of their inherent speaking ability.

That's where I knew her best—in her classroom. Charlotte Jaynes served for decades as the speech teacher at Bossier High School in Bossier City, Louisiana, where Jan Cowart, Mike Wood, and I all attended.

I'm not certain if Mike Wood ever took a course in speech with Miss Jaynes, but Jan Cowart did study under her and I took every course that Miss Jaynes taught. She was that excellent at what she did.

After I graduated with Jan and Mike and 261 other seniors, almost immediately I began using lessons I had learned in Miss Jaynes's speech classes. At Louisiana State University, I auditioned for a disc jockey position at the campus radio station, WLSU. Either I was good, or they were desperate, because the following day I was on the air.

Within two years, I became the general manager of that radio station. Later I was an announcer at WLBI, near Baton Rouge in Denham Springs, and was offered a summer internship at KWKH Radio in Shreveport. After graduating from LSU, I accepted a full-time position at a highly respected radio station, KWKH-AM, and sister station KROK-FM, in Shreveport, across the Red River from Bossier City. Fifty-thousand-watt KWKH is one of the oldest radio stations in the United States. KWKH was home to the historic *Louisiana Hayride*, which was broadcast all over the country. Elvis Presley got his start there.

At KWKH, I worked during the day copywriting and recording commercials, and often doing an on-air shift on weekends. At KROK, a Top 40–format station, I hosted a four-hour show called *The Morning After* each Monday through Friday for four hours, beginning at six in the morning. Even then, many, many times during those days I thought back and silently said, *Thank you, Miss Jaynes.*

Within five years of graduating from Bossier High, I accepted a position at the CBS affiliate KSLA-TV, Channel 12, in Shreveport. For about a year, I worked at KROK Radio in the mornings and KSLA-TV for the remainder of the day. It was a grueling schedule, but I was young, ambitious, and tireless.

Those fast-track media jobs had their seeds planted in Charlotte Jaynes's speech classes. Even though I had no idea of my future employment, I absorbed her lessons on phraseology, inflection, pacing, tone, and a host of other speech components. Later, I realized how important that was to good broadcasting.

Charlotte Jaynes did something else just as important: She influenced me to study and excel in what I did. She often reminded us students that mediocrity wasn't an achievement. Now, all these years later, I can sincerely state that no single person had more to do with my success as a broadcaster than Miss Jaynes.

Within a few years of completing Miss Jaynes's speech classes at Bossier High, imagine my shock and feelings of supreme honor when she invited me back to speak to her classes about careers in broadcasting. When I walked down the halls of BHS, I couldn't have imagined that one day she would ask me to come back as a guest lecturer. That's also when I learned that she regularly listened to me on KWKH. She'd also seen me on KSLA-TV.

I wasn't just returning as the guest of Charlotte Jaynes; it was also a way for me to show my deep appreciation for a woman who cared about me. She was indeed the greatest influence on why I was returning as a guest lecturer.

As I stood to share that morning, I had flashbacks about being in the very same classroom years before. I could still hear her addressing us students from the back of the classroom, "Approach the lectern with boldness, confident in your message."

Miss Jaynes hardly ever sat at her teacher's desk in front of the class. Instead, she chose the back of the classroom, where she could listen to our speeches and critique them.

Any number of times when students spoke, her voice called out from the back of the room, "If I can't hear you back here, neither will your audience. Speak up!"

Another thing I appreciated about her—more later than during those high school years—was her remarkable ability to identify her students' gifts and help them accentuate them.

Few of us went on to become successful professional speakers.

After all, for most students, these speech classes were electives. But, as she reminded us, regardless of our employment choices, all of us needed to communicate clearly.

And those of us who listened and learned benefited enormously from her instruction and wisdom.

Honing my skills in her speech classes was crucial to being successful so early in my career. Indeed, I realized from the start that the ability to communicate in proper English was a critical component of the calling that I would follow my entire life: becoming a professional speaker. And that is exactly what has happened—with special help from Charlotte Jaynes.

In the broadcasting industry, I found a home, first as a disc jockey, a commercial spokesperson, a newscaster, and an actor. In 1985, I made the transition to full-time ministry and preached as often as four times every week.

Some things significantly differed in the 1960s when compared to the second decade of this century. Among those were the occasionally blurred lines between the spiritual lives of students and educators in the context of the public educational system. Frankly, in a lot of school systems in America, faculty members and students are still perfectly comfortable, even happy, to share their beliefs. No proselytizing, no undue influence, and no attempts to convert. And yet, we can't very well be human if we don't share our humanity.

My fellow 1968 Bossier High graduate and also a pastor, Reverend David Melville, and I recently spoke about our speech teacher, Miss Jaynes. It's always great to get another perspective on a person whom we both admire from our past. I was truly taken aback when he began to use the same terms I did to describe her. Bossier High School was very much a public school, but David and

I also attended a college in South Louisiana that is predominately Roman Catholic. We had many college and high school friends who went to parochial schools.

During our time in high school, the Shreveport-Bossier area had an all-boys Catholic school, Jesuit High School, and an all-girls Catholic school called St. Vincent's Academy. In 1968, most of the faculty members were priests and nuns.

David's take on Miss Jaynes was that "she was the nun (teacher) that we never had." He meant that in the most affirming way. David also described her as grandmotherly even though she was only in her mid-forties when we were her students. Or maybe, he said, she was our benevolent-but-serious, loving aunt.

David told me that to this day he gives Miss Jaynes credit for his grammar skills. I smiled when he told me that his quite-intelligent, Harvard-educated son defers to his dad on grammar-related questions. "And I defer to Miss Jaynes."

Like me, David greatly admired Charlotte Jaynes, not only because we learned timeless speaking and writing truths from her. More than the lessons, we knew she cared about each of us and she was serious about life lessons in and out of the classroom at dear old BHS.

Occasionally her faith and active practice of it slipped into conversations in and out of the classroom. Most of the students knew about her role as a director for outside community theatrical productions, many of them Christian-based plays. Some students even appeared in those productions at churches or in community venues.

Acting brought me back to my abiding appreciation for the skills that Charlotte Jaynes had taught me and so many other young people in her illustrious career.

In that capacity, she cast me in a small role as the Lord Chief Justice in our senior play in 1968: the venerable murder mystery *Night Must Fall*, written by Emlyn Williams in 1935.

Like many kids, my first time in front of an audience as an actor, if you want to call it that, I wore a bathrobe and played one of the wise men in a Christmas pageant in 1956 at Waller Elementary. I recall little of those days, but once Miss Jaynes put me in a "real" play, I was hooked.

For more than six decades I have, as theater people say, "trod the boards." Rehearsals for all productions, big or small, are often tedious and boring. During rehearsals, actors may need to repeat one scene a dozen times. Meanwhile, other cast members are often sitting around waiting to go on in the next scene.

In high school, during those long waiting periods, Miss Jaynes and I had our most serious discussions about faith. One of them stands out. As I recall, there were some technical issues holding up the rehearsal that afternoon. Typical of most amateur productions, there was an air of panic by the cast and crew since we were to open in a matter of days.

Miss Jaynes was flustered and barely managed to conceal her frustration. I was sitting near her in the auditorium seats along with the rest of the cast who weren't in the scene currently being rehearsed.

When told there would be another delay while the technical crew worked on lighting issues, she buried her head in her script for perhaps a minute and then looked directly at me, the Lord Chief Justice in the play. Her grimace slowly dissolved into a smile as she beheld a seventeen-year-old man-boy in an old English powdered wig.

She picked up her knitting from the auditorium seat beside her.

In addition to her well-known hobbies of reading and cooking, she was an avid knitter. Our director started knitting furiously as if to defuse her utter exasperation.

Seemingly out of the blue, she paused and peered over her ever-present horn-rimmed glasses and asked me, "Have you been baptized yet?"

"Yes, ma'am. Remember I told you it was in May."

"Oh, now I remember. I'm so proud for you and proud of you. Becoming a Christian is the most important thing a young person can do." She paused before adding, "At this stage of your life, about to graduate, going off to college, it's important to be firmly grounded in your faith. Temptations are about to come at you like never before."

Sitting in our high school auditorium, where I had previously spoken from the stage many times, I was suddenly aware that the words Miss Jaynes was sharing with me about my salvation would be words I would never forget.

We talked about Jesus in quiet moments in the hall between classes and after school when I stayed for Thespian Club meetings (I had been elected vice president of the drama club and Charlotte Jaynes was our faculty advisor). And now as my high school career was counting down to only a few weeks following our senior play, I can only suppose that she felt the freedom to talk about that issue at the center of my life, my faith.

It was as if she knew that because I had come to Christ later than most teens in my church, I needed extra encouragement. She knew that coming to Jesus before graduating from high school would be the crucial factor on whether I made it through college without going astray.

That was a turbulent time in American history—the late sixties. The era of the Vietnam War. Rampant drug use. Rock-and-roll counterculture. Free love. Assassinations. Above all, we were the Woodstock generation, the "turn on, tune in, drop out" generation.

Miss Jaynes couldn't have been more perceptive about what I was about to face. I confess without reservation that, deprived of even the fledgling foundation of my faith in Christ, I would have collapsed in a matter of weeks under the assault of temptations that college offered.

And I did fail.

Sometimes in my dorm room late at night, I cried out for forgiveness for giving in to those temptations. I yearned for guidance and peace. In those dark hours, I often remembered the faces of my pastor, Damon Vaughn, and my Christian friends. Or I'd focus on my Bible study teacher at First Baptist in Bossier City, Joe Cobb, and my youth pastor, Tom Cole. And Charlotte Jaynes. Always Miss Jaynes, to whom I owed so much.

She had taught me how to communicate effectively. The most important point I carried inside my heart was that a speech "begins the moment you leave your seat. Even before you've said your first word, the audience has already begun to form an opinion about you." I can still see her staring right at me when she said those words.

That's not all. Miss Jaynes taught me how to organize my thoughts and present them in a clear, cohesive, and convincing manner.

Even then, it was obvious that Miss Jaynes was serious about her faith, not in a grandstanding fashion, but in a quietly confident way. Her witness impressed me greatly because I knew it was genuine—that it came from a caring heart. Although I couldn't have put it into words as a teenager, later I realized I had been in the presence of greatness—the kind of greatness that God honors. As an educator of young people, she was a living example of a faithful follower of Jesus.

Most of us have special teachers in our lives, and I've been fortunate to have several. Yet I can honestly state that few have ever had the impact like Miss Jaynes in helping to determine who I am. Her consistent following of Christ set the example and standard for me.

Few educators were as beloved as Charlotte Jaynes in the Bossier school system because few directly impacted as many students as she did.

I can't help but wonder what kind of grade I'd get from her on what you've read in this chapter thus far. She certainly wouldn't like the content. It's about her, and she never wanted public praise, no matter how well deserved.

It's a little late, but here it is for public reading.

———

In February 1983, Miss Jaynes and three of her close friends were traveling by car to a wedding in West Texas when a twenty-year-old drunk driver hit their car, killing all four women. It was a truly sad day for me when I got the news.

In the same funeral home where Mike Wood's service had been conducted, Rose-Neath, mourners filled the seats, lined the walls, and packed the lobby. Funeral directors estimated at least four hundred mourners gathered for Charlotte Jaynes's funeral service.

In his memorial message, the pastor of Miss Jaynes's beloved First Presbyterian Church of Bossier City told us that Charlotte Jaynes exhibited the same lifelong dedication to Bossier Parish

Schools that she showed in her Christian walk. "She touched thousands of lives," he said, "in a meaningful and positive way."

She had certainly touched mine.

"She was taken in the twinkling of an eye," he said, quoting a phrase from 1 Corinthians 15:52.

Years later, that would be my same testimony. Last breath here, next breath there.

"God has called her home." The pastor concluded his eulogy by saying, "We're thankful for her life and faith."

Praise God, so am I.

Outside the funeral chapel, the Bossier Parish Schools superintendent, Jap Gullatt, said of her, "She was a truly dedicated teacher whose life was dedicated to her students. Her death is a tremendous loss to the school system."

A former speech student of hers and at that time Waller Elementary School principal, Kent Seabaugh, said, "She was a friend to the teachers and the students. She didn't just touch your life. She impacted it."

And, I must say, to those who loved her, *impact* is an apt description.

When another person's poor driving skills claimed my life in a head-on collision on an East Texas highway only six years later, I immediately stood at the gates of heaven. There among those rushing toward me and greeting me was Miss Charlotte B. Jaynes. We weren't on a stage anymore, in a classroom again, in the hallways of my alma mater, or at a rehearsal. There's no rehearsal for this life—it was the real thing.

When I arrived at the gates, Charlotte didn't listen to me give a speech. She knew that I was coming that day and had anticipated my arrival.

What a splendid reunion we had on January 18, 1989, Charlotte and Don together again. While on earth, we enjoyed a teacher-student, director-actor, and a former teacher–successful graduate relationship. In heaven, those differences disappeared, and we embraced as brother and sister in Christ.

Before I became a Christian, I was greatly impressed by her faith. Her support after I became a Christian sustained me. Her greeting me at the gates assured me that I was home.

If I were standing in front of her right this minute, here's what I would say: "Thirty-five years since you went to heaven, Miss Jaynes, and I'm still preaching every week. I'm still trying to make you proud every time I rise to speak." I'd probably pause long enough to wipe joyful tears from my eyes.

"Now I'm letting the world know that you were instrumental in my getting to heaven. You didn't start me on the road, but you helped me stay faithful and committed. Your faith taught me more than any textbook ever could. You helped me walk a straighter path on my way to heaven. And because of you and the others, I'm trying to get as many people as I can into heaven, too."

I'd most certainly grin and add, "I can hardly wait to see my report card from you."

The Questions on
Everyone's Minds

Chapter 13

Who Will Meet Him?

Over the years I've been asked many questions about heaven. Most of them come from individuals who have anxiety about a person or a situation. For example: I've been asked about cremation, suicide, people of other faiths, animals. How do these decisions and creatures impact heaven?

None of those questions are foolish, because the inquirers truly want to know the answers. Even though I've sometimes had to hold back a smile, I remind myself that the person is seriously asking.

Of the questions I receive, most of them involve my experience with heaven. That makes sense because they connect with me and understand where I'm coming from. They trust me and want me to respond. I feel deeply honored over each question.

In 2006, I led a year-end remembrance service north of Houston at Forest Park, a funeral home in The Woodlands, for families who had lost a loved one during that year. Those families had attended local grief recovery support groups throughout that year. Even though several funeral homes had purchased *90 Minutes in Heaven* in bulk to give away to grieving loved ones, this was one of the few times when it didn't seem appropriate to supply copies of my books for purchase. But I did sign many personal copies that evening.

After that poignant service, I met families in the lobby and spoke to many of them for several minutes. Their stories, all involving the loss of a loved one, were still fresh in their hearts.

"I'm sorry for your temporary loss," I said to one family.

The startled wife looked at me. "Temporary? He's gone—permanently."

"Yes, but you have a reservation in heaven, don't you?" When she nodded, I added, "You'll join him. That's why I call it temporary. The separation is real, but it won't last."

Tears filled her eyes and she hugged me. "I needed that reminder."

Every family had something different to say, and I tried to respond to their specific need. Tears, smiles, and praises filled the atmosphere.

But one experience touched me deeply. I don't remember the name of the woman in her thirties, but she told me she had lost her only child, a boy named Travis.[1]

"We weren't Christians this time last year," she said. "Both Travis and I became believers only a short time before—before..."

"I understand," I said softly, realizing how painful it was for her to talk about her loss. I can't put it into words, but I sensed she wanted to say more or at least needed someone to listen to her.

---

1   I told this story in a different form in *Daily Devotions Inspired by 90 Minutes in Heaven* (New York: Berkeley Praise: 2006), pages 5–9.

She told me a horrible story of an enormously dysfunctional family life prior to her salvation—a life of alcohol, drugs, and atrocious living conditions. It was so awful that one night she took her son, Travis, and left. They found refuge in the lobby of a church during a worship service. That's where their new life began. Before long, both became believers and were baptized.

"You want to tell me what happened to Travis?"

The smile on her face assured me I had asked exactly the right question.

"Travis went to a birthday party for his friend Justin. They were in the same Bible study class at church. It was the first invitation to a birthday party my son had ever received. They even had a swimming pool."

As she continued her story, she broke down several times, but finally, she finished the rest of the story.

"Travis had such a wonderful time at the party, but especially swimming and playing in the pool. Police believe that later that same night, Travis sneaked out of the house and went to the pool."

Then the sobs came as if she had been holding them back. Her last words were, "They found his body the next morning."

After she recovered enough to speak, she said, "I need to ask you something."

The tension on her face made me realize how intent she was. I patted her hand and said as gently as I could, "You're obviously deeply hurt by your loss. What's troubling you?" And then I waited.

It took perhaps thirty seconds before she raised her head and looked directly at me. "Travis drowned. And he was a Christian—"

"I'm sorry for your temporary separation—"

She stared at me as the words sank in. "Yes, yes, it is temporary, isn't it?"

"Indeed, it is," I said.

"But—but Travis became a believer a few months before he died."

"That must have been a great comfort to you," I said.

"My comfort is that Travis and I—both of us—were able to turn to the Lord before—"

Her voice broke and I waited until she could speak again.

"I'm sorry—"

"That's not the main reason I'm crying. You mentioned all the wonderful people who met you at the gates and what a glorious reunion you had with them—"

"Yes, it was powerful."

"My tears are because Travis didn't know any Christians who died before he did. As I listened to you tonight, my heart broke thinking that no one was there to meet him."

Her insight took my breath away. To lose your only son and think of his arriving at the gates of heaven with no one there to greet him! After all, I had been greeted by dear souls who had helped me get to heaven. Instantly, the Holy Spirit spoke very clearly to me and I shared what I heard. "I can assure you that Travis wasn't alone when he entered heaven."

"Do you really think so?"

"Yes, I do. Even if there were no friends or relatives to greet him."

She stared at me, confused.

"If there wasn't anybody he knew at the gates," I said, "Jesus came and met him. Our Savior wouldn't let Travis stand alone at the gate, because he *knew* Jesus. Jesus is the reason that Travis is there."

Her face brightened. "I felt so concerned—his being all alone—"

"In heaven, no one is ever alone. Never. Not ever," I assured her.

"Oh, thank you! Yes, yes, that makes sense. Jesus met him even if no one else was there."

"And if he has Jesus—"

"That's enough, isn't it?"

"I can't think of anything better."

Chapter 14

The Why Questions

Since the release of my first book, thousands of questions have emerged, mostly about heaven. I understand that. I had a large number of questions about heaven before the truck hit me. I'm not certain that I have any fewer questions afterward. But I am much more confident in the answers that I do have.

No one has asked the why questions more often than I have. In *90 Minutes in Heaven*, I wrote an entire chapter on the topic. I've been asking myself those questions since my consciousness returned after the accident.

Although I mentioned this earlier in the book, for a long time I sought the answer to two why questions: Why did God make me come back to this world? And once I was back, why wasn't I healed completely?

Now, thirty years later, I'm still reflecting on the why questions. I don't have all the answers, and I'm sure I never will on this earth. In *90 Minutes in Heaven*, I closed with a final chapter, "The Why Questions," because I had serious difficulty in explaining what happened. That book was published nearly fifteen years after the accident, and another fifteen years have passed since it went to press.

When I wrote that book with my writing partner, Cec Murphey, frankly, I had more questions than answers about why the wreck took place, and why I survived it and what that all meant for my future.

My questions included:

- Why did I die in the car wreck?
- Why did I have the unique privilege of going to heaven?
- Why was I able to only glimpse heaven before being sent back?
- Why did I nearly die several more times in the hospital?
- Why has God let me live in constant pain since January 18, 1989?

From my perspective, here's one obvious conclusion. Simply put, all suffering and pain are consequences of the curse of evil unleashed by humanity's disobedience to God. The "rain falls on the just and the unjust" (Matthew 5:45). *All* of us suffer at various times of our lives, and not just physically. I accept that, knowing full well that there is a place called heaven where I will live forever free of all pain or suffering, or even death.

But that still doesn't answer why God allowed me to glimpse heaven and then return. One thing that I've certainly learned since I came back is that there are people who aren't going to believe me, no matter what I say. They're kin to those of Jesus' day who couldn't acknowledge the truth when Jesus' friend Lazarus was brought back to life after being dead four days. They were the skeptics who refused to see the scores of dead who were spontaneously resurrected in Jerusalem when our Lord died on the cross.

They didn't believe that Jesus was resurrected and was seen by at least five hundred people after His crucifixion. Here's what Paul writes: "He was raised on the third day according to the Scriptures, and he appeared to [Peter], and then to the Twelve. After that, he appeared to more than five hundred of the brothers and sisters at the same time…then he appeared to James, then to all the apostles" (1 Corinthians 15:4–7).

I'm aware that some people don't believe that I was resuscitated that day on the bridge after seeing the gates of heaven. They find ways to refute the heroic measures that sustained me and even saved me while I was in the ICU. They choose not to trust my word (or check into hospital records) about my infectious isolation during my months-long hospitalization.

I don't argue. I can do nothing for them except to stand and say, "I know what happened to me. Your unbelief doesn't take away from the reality of my experience." With all my heart, *I know* I saw heaven. That's why I can testify that it's real—and in some ways more real than the joy and pain that this world could ever offer.

In the 1943 Academy Award–winning movie *Song of Bernadette*, a skeptic asks a monsignor if anyone could believe in miraculous cures. His reply: "For those who believe in God, no explanation is necessary. For those who do not, no explanation will suffice."

Do the skeptics need me to verify my experience? Is there any way I could convince everyone?

No.

I've discovered—sadly—in the years since my accident, many don't read the Bible or believe it's the Word of God. I can't change them.

Often, they have such prejudices against anything religious, especially the Christian faith. I pause to think of the skeptics in the time of Noah's ark. None of his friends and neighbors believed him. After all, there had never been rain on the earth, so how could it possibly rain for forty days?

But sometimes—and I'm always gratified to learn of such

experiences—skeptics pick up a book like this one. Or they attend a speaking event at a civic center, in a high school auditorium, or under a tent. That's when I feel joy—and the obligation—to share the glorious truth about overcoming overwhelmingly painful circumstances in this life.

I've staked my life on one significant fact: I share Jesus' love as the only way, the only truth, and the only life (see John 14:6).

I can't explain everything—even now—but I went to heaven and God thrust me back on earth for a purpose. Perhaps more than one.

Many times, I've wept while talking to individuals, reading letters or e-mails, listening to phone calls from dear folks who do understand. Several of those conversations have included words like these: "I hope you're not still asking about why you're here. Your books, your testimony, or your movie led my husband [or my niece, my mother, or my best friend] to Jesus. I know he's going to heaven now. You bring hope to hurting people."

The statement that touches me most is something like this: "Thank God," they'll say, "that He sent you back."

I have a mission and I believe that's why God has kept me on earth. My body is a physical mess and I never have a day without pain—all day long. That's not a complaint, only an explanation of my situation. My mission is to do whatever I can to point every human soul to Jesus.

I'm still alive to remind and to urge believers that we're here to help everyone get to heaven. Sometimes I stare believers right in the eye and ask, "Who is going to be there because of you?"

Another part of the why answer is that I'm here to send a warning to the world. I wish I could shout and be heard by every human voice, "There's danger ahead in the darkness! Stop going the wrong way! Turn around. Turn to Jesus!"

One day I'll take my last breath here, and my next breath will be in heaven.

When that happens, I'll be in the presence of those who went before me. They'll have met me at the gates. The same people who greeted me will rush out to embrace me again. But this time, I yearn for the times when I can be one of those greeters—when I'm able to rush out to hug the dear ones whom I helped reach heaven.

In my heart, I can already hear them say, "Don, thanks for helping me get here!"

I may not be able to fully answer the why questions, but I'm satisfied with what I know now.

———

My writing partner has said many times that he rarely asks the why question. Here's part of his answer: To ask why becomes an analytical and often intellectual question. Even if God gave me five reasons, it wouldn't change anything.

My accident would have taken place; I would have still gone to heaven for a brief period and returned to earth in a broken body.

Cec suggests it's easier and more tangible to ask the *what* question: What did I learn from the accident and my three decades since? What has being a temporary survivor of death taught me?

It comes out the same. And I'm more convinced than ever that God spared me, even in my badly broken and worn-out body, to witness of His grace and love.

Please meet me at the gate, will you? There are many of you and only one of me. I may not meet you *here*, but I dearly want to meet you *there*.

Chapter 15

Why Did God Take My Loved One?

Legions of people, even devoted followers of God, have been frustrated or angry with God for heart-rending losses suffered in this life. How often have I heard these words as tears cascaded down cheeks?

Here are typical questions that come at me in several ways.

- She was only a child. She had her whole life in front of her and now she's gone. Why?
- Now that he's gone, why would I want to live?
- Why did my mother have to leave me now?
- Why did God take my son?

Once a man asked, "Why did God take my wife? We'd been married only a year and then she was run over by a drunk and died."

I replied, "Would you want your wife to leave heaven to come back to this world?"

While the man hesitated, I said, "It's natural for you to miss her. It would be sad and strange if you didn't. But think about *her* and where she is now. She is in a better place—a perfect place."

Sometimes during question-and-answer times, I ask, "Do you believe God has lost control of the world He created? He still reigns! And each of those loved ones were gifts from God." I believe those words. Our loved ones were God's first; He *loans* them to us. Our painful separation now will be nothing compared to the joyful reunion we'll experience when we're united with them. It is my firm conviction that in heaven we won't remember that we were separated by death on earth. The people in heaven are expecting us even now and there is no time there. Therefore, when we arrive, there will be no literal elapse of time since they arrived. In heaven, our reunion with loved ones is the ultimate beginning of forever!

Often, I point out that righteous Job has already told us, "Mortals, born of woman, are of few days and full of trouble" (Job 14:1).

And who would know better than Job?

"For what is your life?" James asks. "It is even a vapor that appears for a little while, then vanishes away" (James 4:14). "In this world you will have trouble," Jesus clearly states (John 16:33). Here on earth our journey is brief, and often characterized by pain, grief, heartache, and worry—you can expect troubles, pain, loss, and death all around us. How we respond is up to us. We can shake our fists at God—it won't bother Him a bit. He's the sovereign Creator of the universe. (As an aside, I believe that God would rather we be angry with Him than ignore Him. If we're angry, it means there's a chance we'll seek His help.)

By contrast, we can focus our entire lives on ourselves and our pain, never looking beyond our own pain.

Sometimes the pain we feel is guilt over not being more loving or more sensitive. Too late we think of the things we should have done or regret actions we took. We allow our human failures to blind us to the blissful joy of those who are now with Jesus.

My writing partner lost his wife, who suffered intense pain for years. "When I miss her," he said, "and I still do—she died in 2013—I say three words to myself: 'No. More. Pain.' She's free and filled with the joy of heaven. My yearning for her is an expression of selfish need."

But why not take such powerful emotions and use them to glorify God? If we feel the need to weep, shouldn't we also be weeping for lost souls? And if we must be angry, can't we be angry at the sins that destroy the lives of so many?

I don't want to minimize the pain and loss we feel when we lose someone we love. Those are normal reactions and very, very real. Feel your pain, your loss. You can learn to accept your grief as well as remind yourself that God has already forgiven any of your failures toward that loved one.

But what if you took that same level of compassion and turned it beyond your personal situation? What if you sincerely prayed, "Loving God, take that yearning for my loved one and turn it outward so I can yearn for others to experience the joy and peace—and ultimately have a home in heaven"?

We can have absolute confidence in the disposition of the souls of the people whom we have lost in Christ. While we can mourn the temporary separation that we'll surely feel, we can also resolve to celebrate the opportunity to shepherd others to heaven. There they get to know our loved ones and rejoice as well. Hallelujah!

And while we're on the subject of weeping, Jesus wept outside of Lazarus' tomb (see John 11:35). The Bible doesn't say this, but since my trip to heaven, I've come to believe Jesus expressed deep sorrow over bringing Lazarus back from heaven, which Lazarus was already enjoying. Jesus knew the perfection of life beyond the grave. Isn't it possible that He wept because Lazarus would have to die again to return to eternal bliss?

After all, Jesus knew what it was like to leave heaven. He came here from there.

Some members of your welcoming committee could be those you point heavenward.

Chapter 16

What About Those Who *Didn't* Meet You at the Gates?

Sometimes I'm asked about the people I knew here on earth before I died in the car wreck and who didn't meet me at the gates of heaven. They died before I did, but I didn't see them there.

Do I believe that those individuals are in heaven? Certainly. Great-Grandma Hattie Kulbeth's (Joe Socks's mother) not greeting me at the gate didn't mean that she wasn't in heaven. To me, it meant that the influence that she had on my life didn't rise to the level of the others who were present to greet me. She was a sweet and caring woman. I saw her quite infrequently and she was infirm during most of that time and unable to communicate well. But she truly loved the Savior and longed for heaven.

The people who personally greeted me at the gates were those who had *a direct spiritual impact for Jesus on my life here*. They represented those living inside the gates. There were many others whom I knew, loved, and admired here on earth whose individual lives didn't influence me in a deep spiritual sense. Even though they might not be at the gates of heaven, I fully expect to see them when it's time for my permanent return to heaven.

And isn't a spiritual sense the most essential kind? The influence of people I met at the gates of heaven had *direct eternal consequences for me*. They helped me get to heaven by their examples, their words, their deeds, and especially, with their prayers.

A number of people have gone to be with Jesus since I came back from heaven. Many of them are as important to my coming to Christ as the ones I greeted there in 1989.

———

I'm tired of funerals here on earth. In these ensuing years, I conducted them for my father-in-law and mother-in-law, Eldon and Ethel Pentecost. Eldon was also a member of the Don Piper Ministries Board of Directors. I saw my father in the ministry, Dr. Damon Vaughn, make his way to heaven's gates in 2005.

Another pastor friend of mine, R. David Terry, died early in his earthly ministry. My own father, Master Sergeant Ralph Piper, answered the final muster in 2011. My dear friend David Gentiles, former chairman of the board of DPM, left us long before we wanted him to go. My sister-in-law Joyce Pentecost, referenced in *90 Minutes in Heaven*, has been in heaven nearly twenty years. Reverend Jay B. Perkins, the beloved retired pastor who replaced me following my accident, and Fred Thompson, the actor who portrayed Jay B. in our movie, are both with Jesus now. And my dear friend Sonny Steed, another member of my board, departed more recently.

There are those who went before me and whose stories we've

just shared, others who've gone since I returned, some who still may precede me there if I stay awhile longer, and certainly others will follow after my death. So many other important friends, colleagues, and family members are now safe in the arms of Jesus since I stood at the gates thirty years ago.

Chapter 17

Why Didn't You See Jesus?

I can't give the answer to that except to say two things. First, I didn't get inside the gates. Once inside, I *know* I would have seen Him face-to-face. But once inside, I don't believe I could have returned to earth. I wouldn't have wanted to return.

Second, I like to think of my time in heaven as a glimpse—a rare and special preview of what's to come. If you see movie trailers or previews of a TV series, you don't see everything—only enough to whet your appetite for more.

That glimpse changed my life back on earth. I didn't see the Lord face-to-face. That comes later. But His presence in heaven was utterly unmistakable.

Elsewhere I refer to the Lamb's Book of Life. Several times in the book of Revelation, Jesus is called by the symbol of the Lamb. In John's day and in the midst of persecution, outsiders wouldn't have understood what such titles meant, but believers knew.

For instance, my favorite reference to Jesus as the Lamb of God appears in John 1:29. John the Baptist "saw Jesus coming toward him and said, 'Look, the Lamb of God, who takes away the sin of the world.'"

In biblical times, a sacrifice was necessary as atonement for sins. If a penitent could afford it, an unblemished lamb was a desirable and appropriate sacrifice. Every year, the high priest offered an animal sacrifice to atone for the sins of the Jewish people. But Jesus, the perfect sacrifice, showed they no longer needed to go through the ritual.

He became God's Lamb, the perfect sacrifice for our sins. He replaced any and all sacrifices to God. He alone can take away the sins of the world. Calling Jesus the Lamb of God signifies His sacrifice for our sins. He paid a debt He did not owe; we owe a debt we cannot pay on our own.

When I arrived in heaven, I saw light—brilliant light stronger and more luminescent than anything on earth—and yet it didn't blind me. At the gates of heaven, I was bathed in that brilliant, pure, overwhelming light. It was awesome. I could *feel* it. Even now when I reflect on that experience, I understand more fully the words of Jesus Himself: "I am the light of the world. Whoever follows me will never walk in darkness, but will have the light of life" (John 8:12).

Not only did I see and feel His presence at the gate of heaven, but I could also see through the small entrance in the thick walls into the great city. Down the radiant boulevard of gold and up a pinnacle in the center of the city are majestic thrones. From them emanates the brightest lights that I have ever beheld.

Immediately, as overjoyed as I was to be in the presence of the sweet welcoming committee, I felt compelled to move through the gate, travel the golden street, climb the hill, fall at the feet of the thrones, and thank God for allowing me to be there.

That's when I was suddenly jolted back to the wreckage of my car, covered with a tarp, with a desperate preacher praying over me.

Did I see Jesus in heaven? No, but it was the next best thing. I basked in the glory of the Lamp of God (see Revelation 21:23).

I also confess that I'm glad that I didn't glimpse my Savior. If I had seen Jesus, I would have lost all will to live after I returned. In the ensuing months of hospitalization, surgeries, excruciating pain, scary prognoses, and crushing uncertainty, if I had seen Jesus face-to-face in heaven and had that taken away from me, I know I wouldn't have survived here. It's what I still enthusiastically anticipate.

When I try to explain what it means to meet my loved ones at the gates of pearl, I feel so inadequate. No matter how many words I use, I don't get close to the actual experience. To walk inside and see the tree of life and the river of life flowing from the throne of God, colors that were millions of times brighter and more glorious than I'd ever seen on earth, and then to have it snatched from me would have been unbearable.

After my return to earth and the various hospital stays, I fought depression. Part of that, naturally, was normal. But what I couldn't say to anyone was, "I want to go back to heaven. Let me go."

My writing partner's mother-in-law had a serious heart attack in the hospital in 1970—long before patients could sign "do not resuscitate" orders. The room was flooded with doctors and they worked on her body until she was breathing again.

Later that day, she said to her doctor, and to the family, "If I go under again, don't bring me back. It was so marvelous, knowing Jesus is waiting for me."

I understand because when those glorious elements faded from me and I awakened in sterile hospital room 2115, I was encircled by whirring machines, IVs, holes in all parts of my body, and un-speakable intrusions. I wanted to go back.

I held on for one reason: Despite all my pain, my depression, and my painful surgeries, *God wasn't through with my life*. I didn't know what God wanted me to do. But I could trust Him even through the suffering.

No, I didn't see the face of Jesus. Yes, one day I will! I'll see Him, not because I'm worthy, but because He loved me and gave His life for me. It won't be a question of being worthy. It will be a matter of the sacrifice of the Lamb who takes away the sin of the world—the Lamb who took away *my sin*.

Then, I shall see Him face-to-face.

Chapter 18

The Most Common Questions I'm Asked

"DID YOU SEE..."

A woman in Lake Charles, Louisiana, waited two hours for me to sign her copy of *90 Minutes in Heaven*. "I just love your book, Mr. Piper." She thrust her book in front of me. "When you were in heaven, did you see Elvis?"

Her deeply earnest expression made me know she was absolutely sincere.

"Those who met me at the gates of heaven were people who helped me get there. So, no, I didn't see Elvis," I said. "That doesn't mean that he's not there. I knew and loved a lot of people prior to my accident who had died and who did not meet me at the gates. I believe they will be inside when I go through the gates. Elvis may very well be inside if he made an authentic commitment to Christ at some point in his life."

"WHAT IF SOMEONE I LOVED ISN'T IN HEAVEN?"

Sometimes I'm asked, "How can I be happy in heaven if my loved one is in hell?"

Many things are a part of our earthly existence that won't be a part of our heavenly existence. That makes me think of my three young grandchildren. When they're happy, it's delirious happiness. When they're hurt, sad, or angry, the tears flow freely and sometimes loudly. As they grow older, they will learn to control those emotions.

In heaven, only happiness and joy are present, never any tears. There is no need for them.

It's hard to imagine complete bliss. In heaven, everything is perfect. For people like me, it means no more physical pain. Just think, no depression, no broken bones, no broken hearts, no cancer, and no surgeries. In heaven, life is unending. We'll live in the presence of God. No funerals, no hearses, no caskets, no mourning, no tears, no death—all banished forever from the city limits of heaven.

Death is an inevitable part of life on planet Earth. The death rate here is 100 percent. If hell is eternal death (and it is), people there will want to cease existing, but instead, they'll experience endless torment and separation from God.

The things that seem to divide us here, such as theological differences, will cease to exist! One God, one heaven, one people, one eternity.

The Bible says that in heaven there will be no sun or moon (see Revelation 22:23). Why would we need external illumination if there is never any darkness? We'll have continuous light, which means no night. In this present life, darkness is something that is undesirable and associated with sin and godlessness. In heaven, there is no darkness, no sin. People won't kill, steal from each other, covet each other's belongings, lie, or cheat. We'll never misunderstand or be misunderstood.

According to Revelation 21:27, "Nothing impure will ever enter it, nor will anyone who does what is shameful or deceitful, but only those whose names are written in the Lamb's Book of Life."

This verse implies two basic truths. There is a way into heaven and there is a way that makes it impossible to enter heaven. The way in is Jesus. He once said to His disciples, "I am the way and the truth and the life" (John 14:6). Without an authentic relationship with Jesus, there simply is no way a soul can enter the kingdom of God.

Those who have rejected the salvation Jesus offers won't be registered in the Lamb's Book of Life—the holy record of all faithful followers of Jesus.

Both Cec and I have our names *on* a lot of books and we are deeply honored, but if you ever wanted your name to appear *in* a book—the Lamb's Book of Life is the one you want to be in. Conversely, without Jesus, there is no hope for salvation, no hope of heaven, no hope of eternal life in the presence of God. Rejecting God leads to death, everlasting separation from Him, and the direct path to hell.

If someone you love does not have their name in the Lamb's Book of Life, run, sprint, crawl, hobble to them, and tell them about Jesus!

"IN HEAVEN, WILL WE KNOW WHO ISN'T THERE?"

I think not. That would lead to tears, sadness, and remorse. Those emotions don't exist in heaven. I believe we'll remember those souls no more. If we remembered the missing souls, we'd be re-morseful for their absence. That's impossible in heaven!

If we do remember those whom we loved and will meet in heaven—and we will—it's just as possible not to remember those we've lost.

The Bible tells us that when we ask forgiveness, "As far as the east is from the west, so far has He removed our transgressions from us" (Psalm 103:12). Micah 7:19 tells us that God "will tread our sins underfoot and hurl all our iniquities in the depths of the sea." Certainly this same God can—and will—remove our remembrance of those who rejected Him.

In heaven, we will indeed be known as we are known, meaning that we will know Him and know each other. God wouldn't want us to pine away over those who aren't there. If we knew who wasn't there, it wouldn't be heaven.

The Bible teaches us that the souls whose rejection of God has condemned them to hell will have an awareness of the reality of heaven (see Luke 16:23–24). Wouldn't that make hell all the more hellish?

Rather than worry or anguish over the spiritual influence that we might have shared with those who seemingly died without Jesus, we can and should use that raw emotion to double our efforts to see that no one else goes to hell!

They might go to hell in spite of our best efforts, but let's make them go around us.

"CAN OUR LOVED ONES SEE US NOW?"

Sometimes, the follow-up question is, "If people in heaven don't know who's not there, can they see what's happening on earth right now?"

I like to point out that, through the years, I've done considerable work on the theatrical stage. I could have been acting superbly, but if no one was in the audience, what's the point?

In high school, I ran track. Bleachers were set up for anyone who wanted to watch the field events. Now, compare that to your life. Would we really want the people in heaven to be in the bleachers observing our every move on earth?

I don't think they do.

Here's another way I approach this: Jesus says in Luke 9:62, "No one who puts a hand to the plow and looks back is fit for service in the kingdom of God." Imagine we're standing in the full glory and majesty of God. How tempted would we be to look back over our shoulders and consider earth? In heaven, are we in the bleachers waving celestial pompoms, cheering on every little earthly victory and groaning over every earthly missed "goal"? I don't think so.

Heaven is about joy—far surpassing any earthly words. Little that happens on earth ever rises to the level of the simplest heavenly activity.

Except for one thing.

In Luke 15, Jesus talks about a lost sheep, a lost coin, and a lost son, and states, "There is rejoicing in the presence of the angels of God over one sinner who repents" (verse 7).

The great God of creation and His holy angels get extremely excited about one single human repenting and embracing Jesus as Savior. Let's make this personal. The exact moment you trusted Christ as Savior, celebration took place in your honor in heaven. Maybe you've had "Happy Birthday" sung to you many times to celebrate your birth on earth. In heaven, the most jubilant singing imaginable is the moment you were born again in Jesus. Now that's a happy birthday!

"Do people in heaven know what is happening here on earth?" We can be certain of one fact. They know when you got saved. If you were a follower of Jesus before they died, they know you're coming. Everyone there knows who's coming. They don't miss you; they expect you!

Chapter 19

Why Doesn't God Take Us to Heaven the Moment We Accept Christ?

When Jesus was dying on the cross, He was flanked by two convicted criminals. Luke 23:32–43 gives us the full story.

One criminal "hurled insults at [Jesus]. 'Aren't you the Messiah? Save yourself and us!'" The other rebuked that man, saying they deserved their punishment, but Jesus had done nothing wrong. He then called out to the Lord, "'Jesus, remember me when you come into your kingdom.' Jesus answered him, 'Truly I tell you, today you will be with me in paradise'" (verses 39, 40–43).

From the mouth of Jesus, "Today you will be with me in paradise." That's how quickly we arrive at the gates of heaven.

Being prepared for what happens next (and something *will* happen next) is the most important thing that we'll ever do. Our very souls depend on it. We're not going to be able to hit the pause button and reconsider.

Not long ago, I stood with a family in the intensive care unit of a Houston hospital. Expensive whirring machines were keeping a man alive.

I've been on life support myself. I don't remember much about it, but that day I was watching a man experience passing away. Loved ones held his hand, stroked his face, whispered to him, and talked in hushed tones to each other.

The purpose of that gathering was to say good-bye. The life support was about to be disconnected. The patient had left a DNR order—do not resuscitate. He didn't want them to artificially sustain his life. When he could no longer breathe or his heart could no longer pump blood on its own, he wanted to pass away.

I have been in many such rooms. Sometimes people weep. On other occasions, I see faint smiles of remembrance. I think of it as a holy moment: A person whom they know and love is about to die.

And that raises the question: Why do we keep living after we become Christians? Wouldn't it save us a lot of trouble and heartache if we just went to heaven the moment we accepted Christ as Savior?

Consider this, however. Since I became a Christian at sixteen years of age and graduated from college and married my college sweetheart, we were blessed with three children. I started a career in broadcasting and then moved into full-time Christian service, all before I got hit by the truck. If I had gone to heaven the moment I got saved in May 1966, I would have missed all of that.

And that doesn't include what happened after January 18, 1989. Other memories fill my heart, such as the day I walked my daughter, Nicole, down the aisle for her wedding. I was present at the college graduations of all three of my children. Today I'm the grandfather of three beautiful children.

If I had gone to heaven at age sixteen, I would have missed so many wonderful experiences that I cherish today.

———

Jesus called His original followers to leave their respective jobs and follow Him for three and a half years. After Jesus went to heaven, they served Him until all were martyred, except John, who was exiled to an island called Patmos, where he apparently died an ordinary death.

Even though they changed occupations, they didn't stop living. Quite the contrary, they would probably testify that their lives never really had meaning until they met Jesus. And so it is.

Yes, I have been with suffering souls who, on their very deathbed, professed belief in Christ and took their next breath in heaven. It's fulfilling and exciting when that happens, but horrifying, too. While we praise God for the new names written in the Lamb's book, the risk of waiting at death's door to make the decision is sad. They missed so much of the joy and peace from living the godly life on earth.

Of course, Jesus wants to save us today. Then we can live for Him and serve Him until He calls us home. *Truly, we are saved to serve.* Most often that means a lifetime of service, not just the moments before death. Some of the most contrite and disappointed believers that I have met are ecstatic over their salvation but deeply remorseful for waiting until they were eighty years old to make that choice.

In some ways, of course, what I've written above is personal. I don't know all the answers to that question, but here's something I sometimes ask: If all believers immediately go to heaven after their conversion, who will be left to spread the message?

We're still here on divine assignment. God has a purpose for us. The fulfillment of that purpose starts with giving ourselves fully to God. Paul writes, "I urge you, brothers and sisters, in view of God's mercy, to offer your bodies as a living sacrifice, holy and acceptable to God. This is your true and proper worship" (Romans 12:1).

This is our purpose.

One of the last things Jesus said to His disciples was, "You will be my witnesses in Jerusalem, and all Judea and Samaria and to the ends of the earth" (Acts 1:8). He meant that they were to tell others about Him—among neighbors and friends. Then, they were to spread the word throughout the entire earth. Tradition tells us that Thomas went to India and proclaimed the gospel.

We're here as witnesses or as divine representatives. Or as Paul put it, "If anyone is in Christ, the new creation has come. The old has gone, the new is here. All this is from God, who reconciled us to himself through Christ and *gave us the ministry of reconciliation*: that God was reconciling the world to himself in Christ, not counting people's sins against them. *And he has committed to us the message of reconciliation. We are therefore Christ's ambassadors, as though God were making his appeal through us.* We implore you on Christ's behalf: Be reconciled to God" (2 Corinthians 5:17–20, emphasis mine).

And there's more. Jesus said: "The harvest is plentiful, but the workers are few. Ask the Lord of the harvest, therefore, to send out workers into his harvest field" (Matthew 9:38). Not only are we representatives of God, but another reason to stay on earth is to pray for others to accept the responsibility of being His witnesses—or as Jesus puts it, His workers. God intends for each one of us to be part of His grand scheme for the world.

Here's one more thing. We call ourselves Christians. *Christ* isn't Jesus' surname, but His title, which means the "anointed one." And we are anointed—appointed, chosen—to bring good news to the world. And that news is simple: "God loves you and wants to live with you forever."

Or we can quote Jesus' words: "Go into all the world and preach the gospel to all nations" (Mark 16:15). Or, "This gospel of the kingdom will be preached in the whole world as a testimony to all nations, and then the end will come" (Matthew 24:14).

While we're still drawing breath on earth, we are here *on* purpose and *for* a purpose. We don't have to give up our occupations as the disciples did, but we have the same calling they did.

Go and tell the world about Jesus! That's your purpose in being here.

———◆———

This chapter began with my standing in the ICU, surrounded by machines and tubes and family members saying good-bye to their loved one. That's where many of us will pass our last earthly moments. The next, we'll be in heaven surrounded by those whom we have loved and lost for just a little while. All of us are only one breath away from heaven.

If heaven is your ultimate home, when your time comes, who will greet you at the gates of heaven? Who will be there because of you? That last question is why you're still here. To draw people to Christ.

Chapter 20

What Happens to Our Bodies in Heaven?

When I made my appearance at the gates, one thing that amazed me was that everyone was healthy and vibrant, whole, and ageless. Not one person was old. It's like the Garden of Eden in which everything and everyone was perfect. I especially remember my grandmother with those sparkling white teeth—something she didn't enjoy on earth after losing them at an early age.

After the entrance of sin, death took place—but it wasn't an immediate, on-the-spot death. Until Genesis 3, Adam and Eve were sinless and ageless.

After their disobedience, God cursed them by expelling them from Eden. He says, "[The man] must not be allowed to reach out his hand and take also from the tree of life and eat, and live forever" (Genesis 3:22). The obvious meaning is that time didn't count during the period of innocence.

Adam lived 800 years after Eden (Genesis 5:4). People lived much longer, from 800 years old to Methuselah's 969 years, before the ages got shorter. By the time Abraham came into the picture, people lived much shorter lives. Abraham lived 175 years (Genesis

25:7); Jacob survived 147 years (Genesis 47:28); and Joseph lived until he was 110 (Genesis 50:26).

Psalm 90, attributed to Moses, reads, "All our days pass away under your wrath; we finish our years with a moan. Our days may come to seventy years, or eighty, if strength endures; yet the best of them are but trouble and sorrow" (verses 9–10).

Psalm 90 shows the ongoing punishment for sin, and every human being on earth dies. But there's great news! Heaven reverses that and takes us back to the innocence and purity of the Garden of Eden.

Think back to a generation after Jesus' death and resurrection. The first disciples were old and obviously some had died. The believers seemed to have no problem with believing in the resurrection. They must have known the accounts I've mentioned above, so their natural questions revolve around their bodies. "What will we look like? Will we have the same bodies?"

Paul devotes a large portion of 1 Corinthians to explain about resurrection bodies. Beginning with 15:35, he answers the question with an analogy. He compares our bodies to seeds. We plant seeds in the ground, they die, and in dying they produce a plant. "But God gives it a body as he has determined" (verse 38).

In a beautiful poetic statement, Paul points out that earthly bodies and heavenly bodies aren't the same (verse 40). His summation statement reads, "So will it be with the resurrection of the dead. The body that is sown is perishable, it is raised imperishable...It is sown a natural body, it is raised a spiritual body" (verses 42, 44).

From Paul's words and from my own experience at the gates of heaven, I can say, we will all have bodies—but not earthly ones. "I declare to you, brothers and sisters, that flesh and blood cannot inherit the kingdom of God, nor does the perishable inherit the imperishable" (verse 50).

"We believe in the resurrection and look forward to it. But what happens to our bodies?" That must have been the major question asked by late-first-century believers. The generation after Jesus saw their older Christian friends dying.

"Christ has been raised from the dead. He is the first of a great harvest of all who have died" (15:20). Older translations refer to Jesus as the "first fruits"—which has an important theological emphasis. When Moses gave the law to the people, one of the requirements involved giving the first produce from their fields and orchards to God. This was taken to the priests, who were God's representatives.

The initial fruit of harvest was meant as a dedication to God. Moses writes, "I give you all the finest new wine and grain they give the LORD as the firstfruits of their harvest. All the land's firstfruits that they bring to the LORD will be yours. Everyone in your household who is ceremonially clean may eat it" (Numbers 18:12–13).

"Put some of the first produce from each crop you harvest into a basket and bring it to the designated place of worship," Deuteronomy 26:2–3 commands. "Go to the priest in charge at that time and say to him, 'With this gift I acknowledge to the LORD your God that I have entered the land he swore to our ancestors he would give us.'"

Leviticus 23:9–11 points out that the waving of the sheaf of the first grain harvest before the Lord served to consecrate the whole harvest that followed. Similarly, the resurrection of Christ is referred to as the first fruits of those who have died and will become the assurance that all who trust Him will be resurrected. Jesus was the first fruit—the beginning of the fulfillment of resurrection for all of us. That implies there will be a bountiful harvest afterward.

Paul's response states, "What Jesus was, we shall be" (1 Corinthians 15:20). The apostle John explains it this way: "Dear friends, we are already God's children, but he has not yet shown us what we will be like when Christ appears. But we do know that we will be like him" (1 John 3:2).

Of course, that's not the full answer to the question. One way to approach this is to look at two of the physical appearances of Jesus after the resurrection. In both instances, He showed Himself to followers—disciples who had traveled with Him and knew Him well. They didn't recognize Him because of what we sometimes refer to as His glorified body—and that same thing will one day happen to us.

In 2018, I was privileged to make another pilgrimage to Israel. In a matter of days I was able to visit the Garden Tomb, the Church of the Holy Sepulcher, the Crusader Church at Emmaus, and the Sea of Galilee. All of those sites were visited by Jesus *after* His resurrection.

Look at the account of Mary Magdalene. On Sunday morning, she runs to the tomb and discovers it's empty. She stands there, crying, because she thinks His body has been taken away and she doesn't know where to look. A man she assumes is the gardener asks why she's crying.

The man is Jesus, and she doesn't recognize Him. "Jesus said to her, 'Mary'" (John 20:16). After Jesus calls her by name, she recognizes Him. From that verse, we infer that Jesus' appearance to Mary was different or she would have known Him immediately.

Then there is the second and stronger story from the Gospel of Luke. Two disciples are walking the seventeen-mile distance from

Jerusalem to Emmaus. They were sad and talking about the things that had taken place, especially the death of Jesus.

A stranger appears and begins walking with them. In those days it was common for people going in the same direction to join together. The stranger, of course, is Jesus, whom they don't recognize. They talk about the things that just happened in Jerusalem.

"What are you discussing together as you walk along?" Jesus asks.

They are surprised He doesn't know about the current events. Immediately, they tell Him about Jesus, who "was a prophet, powerful in word and deed before God and all the people" (Luke 24:19).

They travel together until just before they reach Emmaus and Jesus starts to turn off, but they beg Him to stay with them, pointing out that it's almost dark. Apparently at an inn, they sit together and eat. During their time together, the Lord reveals Himself and they're "startled and frightened, thinking they saw a ghost" (verse 37).

Although not as dramatic, recorded in John 21:1–4, Jesus stands at the Sea of Galilee while Peter, James, and John go fishing and catch nothing. From the shore, Jesus yells to them, "Throw your net on the right side of the boat and you will find some" (verse 6). John then recognizes Jesus—perhaps from His voice—and tells Peter, "It is the Lord!" (verse 7).

From these accounts in the Bible, we learn that our resurrection bodies will retain our identities and that others can recognize us, although we'll possess greater capabilities than we have with our present earthly bodies. From my trip to heaven, I can testify to that. I recognized everyone—even though most of them were at a different age than when I'd last seen them.

Chapter 21

Do We Become Angels in Heaven?

One evening during the Q&A after a talk I'd given, a young woman asked if we become angels in heaven. Several people snickered, and she obviously heard them. She hurriedly added, "When I was in fourth grade, my classmate Bobby was hit by a bus when he tried to run across the street. At his funeral, one of the speakers said, 'God needed another angel in His heavenly choir and He chose Bobby.'"

"I don't know where the speaker got that information," I responded, "but it's not in the Bible. If we turn into angels, I wouldn't have recognized anyone at the gates who welcomed me. They were all human—totally human."

It amazes me when I occasionally meet people who think we're transformed into heavenly hosts. I have no idea where they get such ideas.

The only verse I can think of that some might misunderstand is Luke 20:36. Jesus said, referring to what happens after the resurrection, "And [humans] can no longer die; they are like the angels." The meaning is that they are like angels in that they'll never die. There's no indication that we're transformed into those heavenly creatures.

Why would we want to be angels? Certainly, angels are glorious messengers with all kinds of amazing powers, but the Bible strongly implies that humans are the zenith of God's creation. Humans alone were created in the image of God (see Genesis 1:27). Jesus' sacrifice tells us that we are the central object of the love of God and His never-ending quest to enjoy fellowship with us.

Angels are eternal beings. When the Lord spoke to Job, He asked, "Where were you when I laid the earth's foundation?... while the morning stars sang together and all the angels shouted for joy?" (Job 38:1–7).

The New Testament, written in Greek, uses *aggelos*, which means "messenger." The Hebrew word *mal'ak* means the same thing. Their primary function is expressed by their name—they're divine messengers.

I firmly believe an angel was holding my right hand, providing me strength and comfort in my gruesome collision. And it was the angels who bore me up to heaven when I died (see Luke 16:22). Let's stop here and notice that the angels are doing the "heavy lifting." That's their role in God's scheme of things. They were ministering to a human being, the enormous object of His love. We don't become angels in heaven. Created in the image of God, we will dine at His table (see Revelation 19:9).

Chapter 22

When Babies Die, Do They Go to Heaven?

One of the most common and difficult questions I hear is about what happens to infants who die. This is more an emotional question rather than a biblical one, especially when asked by a parent who has lost a young child.

Emotionally, we want to yell, "Yes! Of course!" but the Bible doesn't make any clear statement; however, we can make some serious inferences. Before I go any further, I want to state that I believe in a loving, compassionate God, and that He is full of mercy and kindness. That, in itself, gives me a positive response about infant deaths.

Part of my answer revolves around the important principle in the Old Testament. Parents were fully responsible for their children. Whatever decisions they made also affected their children. In the New Testament, this is brought out clearly in Acts 16:16–40. Paul and Silas were imprisoned at Philippi and in the middle of the night, "Suddenly there was such a violent earthquake that the foundations of the prison were shaken. At once all the prison doors flew open, and everyone's chains came loose" (Acts 16:26).

The jailer "rushed in and fell trembling before Paul and Silas" (verse 29). He asked the great question: "Sirs, what must I do to be saved?" (verse 30).

The once-chained apostles replied, "Believe in the Lord Jesus, and you will be saved—you and your household" (verse 31). This jailer and his family became the first Gentiles to come to Christ!

We believe that the only way to be saved is through Christ. It is a fact that with no Savior, no one can have eternal life.

———

What happens to infants, fetuses, or even young children the moment they die? What about those who are aborted? Where do they go after death? God has said that all humans are born into sin, but they certainly don't go to hell, do they?

For anyone who has ever lost a baby or knows someone who has lost one, what can we say to them? Is there anything in the Bible that might provide us with words of hope and comfort about their great loss of an infant? Grieve with them, cry with them, and express your sorrow for their loss. And that's all that anyone can really say.

Most theological teachers believe that those children who die in infancy are numbered among the redeemed. That is to say, we have a certain level of confidence that God will be particularly gracious toward those who have never had the opportunity to be exposed to the gospel, such as children, infants, or fetuses. Or another way to say it is that they died before they were old enough to choose salvation provided by Jesus.

This is only an analogy, but it satisfied me: In the Old Testament, God refused to let the disobedient Israelites enter the

Promised Land because of their lack of faith. He didn't, however, hold the children responsible for what the parents had done. "And the little ones that you said would be taken captive, your children, who do not yet know good from bad—they will enter the land. I will give it to them and they will take possession of it" (Deuteronomy 1:39).

The prophet Isaiah writes the now-famous passage about the virgin bearing a son and adds, *"Before the boy knows enough to reject the wrong and choose the right*, the land of the two kinds you dread will be laid to waste" (Isaiah 7:16, emphasis mine).

In the New Testament, people brought their children to Jesus to ask Him to lay hands on them and bless them. In one account, Jesus' zealous disciples rebuked the people.

"When Jesus saw this, he was indignant. He said to them, 'Let the little children come to me, and do not hinder them, for the kingdom of God belongs to such as these'" (Mark 10:14). That verse seems clear to me, especially these words: for the kingdom of God belongs to such as these—the innocent.

Although I can't provide what's called proof texts, I refer to the grace and love of God, and remind myself that He doesn't provide answers to every question we may have.

My final response is this: "The secret things belong to the LORD our God, but the things revealed belong to us, and to our children forever, that we may follow all the words of this law" (Deuteronomy 29:29).

I believe the grace and benevolence of God is far, far greater than we humans can imagine.

Chapter 23

A Personal Response About Babies Who Die

In the previous chapter, I tried to answer the general question about children who die. This chapter is my personal response.

When Eva and I married in 1973, we had already talked about having children. Two boys and two girls seemed ideal.

After Eva's graduation from college and a year and a half into our marriage, we prayerfully decided that maybe it was time to start a family. I look back at these decisions like getting married, having a certain number of kids, and when to have them, and realize the gravity of those events now in a way that I could never have understood then.

Eva and I were in love. We thought that since 1976 would be the bicentennial of our country, it would be historic to try and have a baby on July 4, 1976. God decided that the perfect historic day to have a baby was June 19, 1976. Angela Nicole Piper made her debut that night about nine o'clock. Even though we had been holding out for July 4, we were ecstatic.

It seemed so easy then to conceive, endure pregnancy, and bring a child home from the maternity ward. About a year and half later, we decided that it was time for baby number two, maybe a boy this time. Eva became pregnant and we told the world.

Everything went smoothly until one night, Eva screamed from the bathroom, "Come quick!"

We lost the baby, and had to tell our friends. Everyone was sympathetic. For a time, we were confused and inconsolable. Then we decided to try again. But this time we decided not to tell anyone.

Nothing happened. Months drifted by and we began to wonder if Nicole would be an only child. If that's what God willed, we told ourselves, we'd accept it. Both of us went to the doctors and were tested to make certain that we were capable of still having children. We were.

Approximately three years after losing the last baby, Eva became pregnant again. We were delighted, but kept it to ourselves for fear of repeating our previous loss. Everything went well until Eva went in for a routine checkup. She called me at my office from the doctor's office: "Come quick; they're checking me into the hospital. I have an ectopic pregnancy." Sometimes called a tubal pregnancy, this is where the fetus develops outside the uterus. It can be critical not only for the baby but also for the mother. It's a common cause of maternal death in the first trimester. Even if the baby survives, irreparable damage can be done to the mother's ability to have more children.

We lost the baby.

We were so heartbroken by the loss and saddened by the possibility of never having brothers and sisters for Nicole. In fact, we considered not risking pregnancy again.

Then Eva became pregnant with twins. Healthy at last. Christopher and Joseph were born five years after their sister. Nicole is forty-two now and the twins are thirty-seven. Praise God, they have their own children.

But what happened to the children we *almost* took home from the hospital? They didn't live long enough to experience life here. They didn't sin and never had the opportunity to hear about Jesus. Is it possible for them to be in heaven? Are there any children in heaven?

All children, born or unborn, are special gifts from God. They were His before they were ours. I believe that He only *loans* us to each other on earth. God is capable of taking good care of these humans in heaven until we are all united with them there. Those unborn children as well as all children, before they reach an age of being able to decide for themselves to have an authentic relationship with God, are taken to Him when they die or are never born. The next time I'll be with them means we'll never be separated again.

In telling this personal account, I do so to comfort and assure those who, like Eva and I, lost babies before they were born, or shortly after birth.

A few intimate friends know that Eva and I lost *three* unborn children because of pregnancy complications. For a young couple, deliriously happy about the prospect of parenthood, these losses were excruciatingly painful. Yet Eva and I have every confidence that those dear souls whom we didn't get a chance to meet and love here on earth will be reunited with us in heaven—just as we will meet those ancestors who came before us, and the saints of the Bible who pointed the way to heaven for us all.

What about those who were separated at birth, given up for adoption, or never had the joy of meeting their earthly families?

It's my conviction that if they're prepared for heaven, they'll join us *inside* the twelve gates.

———

Here's a story from the Bible that brought comfort to me after our losses. King David fathered several children, including one with his wife Bathsheba, even though the baby was conceived when she was married to someone else.

David and Bathsheba's baby boy was born sickly. King David prayed over the infant, pleading with God for the child to survive. After seven days of life, the boy died.

Those in the king's court were devastated and feared that David might fall into deep depression. Instead, David got up, bathed, changed his clothes for the first time in a week, and went into the house of the Lord and worshiped.

Servants around him were confused to see the abrupt change in their king. "While the child was alive, you fasted and wept, but now that the child is dead, you get up and eat!" (2 Samuel 12:21).

Here are King David's words, written as a father, not a king: "While the child was still alive, I fasted and wept. I thought, 'Who knows? The LORD may be gracious to me and let the child live.' But now that he is dead, why should I go on fasting? Can I bring him back again? *I will go to him but he will not return to me*" (verses 22–23, emphasis mine).

Those words have comforted and encouraged fathers and mothers and many others across the centuries since they were uttered. They also brought comfort to me.

"I will go to him." I've been to King David's tomb in Jerusalem. He died and was buried. He is not there. He's with God the Father.

And I believe that David's son is there with his father. Is the boy still a baby? Maybe. Maybe not.

God loves us even before we are born; He loves those who weren't born. I believe that God loves all aborted babies. And He certainly loves us after we're born and before we're able to understand our sin and rebellion against Him (sometimes called the age of accountability). He also loves those who never reach the mental capacity of an adult.

I find no evidence in the Bible that children will still be children in heaven. Remember, Adam and Eve were never children. That's how God chose to create the first humans. Maybe that's His template for heaven as well. A few times I've heard people say that everyone in heaven will be thirty-three years old since that's how old Jesus was when He was crucified. There is no evidence of stages of life, i.e., infancy, adolescence, adult, or elderly in heaven. I believe that stages of life happen only on earth. We'll find out, won't we?

Did I see any babies or children in heaven? No. That doesn't mean they're not there. Here are two reasons for my answer. First, my greeters in heaven were the people who helped me get there or encouraged me along the way. No babies ever did that. Second, I firmly believe that all my children living and dead were His before they were mine. He only loans our children to us. For that matter, He only loans us to each other. He's taking good care of the ones I haven't met yet.

I believe my unborn children are waiting just inside the gates. And whether they're infants or children in heaven, we're all brothers and sisters anyway. The moment I embrace them, I'll know them, and we can begin our eternal lives together. No birth and death in heaven.

God's love assured me of a reunion with my children in heaven. I continue to find comfort in the words of David, "I will go to him."

Chapter 24

Will There Be Pets in Heaven?

Of all the questions I get asked, this is one of the most emotional ones: Will my dog or my cat be with me in heaven?

I always respond with, "I didn't see any animals, but I was still outside the gates and ready to move inside when I was prayed back to earth. I can only express my opinion."

Cec usually answers by pointing out that the Bible doesn't speak about our pets in heaven. There are significant historical and theological reasons for that.

Dogs and cats weren't generally domesticated in biblical times. Cats are never mentioned in the Bible and dogs only in negative ways. In those days, dogs were scavengers. So why would there be any reference to pets when the Bible focuses on heaven?

Today we use the word *scavengers* to refer to creatures like houseflies, hyenas, or vultures that feed on dead or decaying matter. We need to remind ourselves that the Bible was written by and for ancient people with references that, for them, would have meaning. We affirm that the Bible was inspired, and its message is timeless, but the culture was neither. The Bible's silence on many things could be an indication that God simply doesn't value those things as highly as we do today.

Adam's very first responsibility was to name the animals and provide for them. After their creation, God has been interested in the well-being of animals. The Bible says that Jesus will return from heaven on a horse (see Revelation 19:11–16).

I believe that if heaven is enhanced by animals, then they will be there, just as He put them here on earth for us.

I love what the eminent scholar, author, and theologian J. I. Packer said when asked about animals in heaven. I served on a "heaven" discussion panel with Packer and Randy Alcorn in Dallas one year. Like Jesus often did, Dr. Packer answered a question with a question: "Madam, would heaven ever be less than this? If you believe that your pet is a great gift from God, I believe that that pet could be in heaven."

Will Rogers said, "If there are no dogs in heaven, then when I die, I want to go where they went." Mark Twain remarked, "Heaven goes by favor; if it went by merit, you would stay out and your dog would go in."

Billy Graham's response to the pet question was, "God will prepare everything for our perfect happiness in heaven, and if it takes my dog being there, I believe he'll be there."

Those four gentlemen come from vastly different realms of life. But they sum up humanity's love of and even preoccupation with animals.

Chapter 25

Rewards in Heaven

"WHY WILL THERE BE REWARDS IN HEAVEN?"

The first time I was asked this question, it came from a long-time believer who had grown weary in working for God. She had been wondering if all the effort really mattered. It didn't surprise me, and I realized it came from a sincere heart. The woman added, "Why would we need rewards in heaven? If we're with Jesus in a perfect world, isn't that enough?"

The phrasing of her question implied an affirmative answer. And yet God does promise rewards. In Revelation 22:12, Jesus says, "Look, I am coming soon! My reward is with me, and I will give to each person according to what they have done." And in 2 Corinthians 5:10 Paul writes, "For we must all appear before the judgment seat of Christ, so that each of us may receive what is due us for the things done while in the body, whether good or bad."

But why? What's their purpose?

My short answer, and probably the most obvious: Does God

ask for and reward faithfulness? All through the Bible we're exhorted to obey, to live godly lives, and above all, we need to remind ourselves of Jesus' answer to the Pharisees. When they asked him to define the greatest commandment in the law, "Jesus replied, 'Love the Lord your God with all your heart and with all your soul and with all your mind.' This is the first and greatest commandment. And the second is like it: 'Love your neighbor as yourself.' All the Law and the Prophets hang on these two commandments" (Matthew 22:37–40).

Paul writes, "Now it is required that those who have been given a trust must prove faithful" (1 Corinthians 4:2).

Doing good won't get anyone into heaven, but a willingness to do good for the Lord in this life will bring us rewards in the next. As Christians, we must make the personal decision on how we live our lives on this earth. We can either choose to fully surrender everything to God and let Him decide our destiny, or we can choose to do things our own way and run our own lives. Too many Christians don't seek God's answer about their vocations or careers. They don't ask God to show them what He wants their goals and aspirations to be. They're also the ones who cry out when they have trouble or seek a miracle in their times of severe need.

By contrast, only God knows what's best for us on all matters. We have no way of knowing what's ahead. God not only knows, but He can and will safely guide us to reach the goals He has set for us. By a system of rewards, God shows that whatever we do is worth it. As I sometimes say, "It all counts." Whatever we do in love and obedience will find reward later.

Especially, think of those who are persecuted for their faith. If getting into heaven is all that matters, why don't those stalwart believers just say, "Kill me"?

The reward comes from standing firm, loving God, and witnessing for our faith. As a young believer, I was deeply impressed the first time I read the story of Stephen, the first Christian martyr. The story is in Acts 7–8.

God used two things from that story to shape my life. First was the courageous witness of Stephen. In his dying moments, "While they were stoning him, Stephen prayed, 'Lord Jesus, receive my spirit.' Then he fell on his knees and cried out, 'Lord, do not hold this sin against them.' When he had said this he [died]" (Acts 7:59). That's the first thing—his faithful witness to Jesus Christ—until the very moment he died.

The second is the next sentence: "And Saul [Paul] approved of their killing him" (Acts 8:1). As we know, shortly after that, Saul has a conversion experience on his way to Damascus. The Bible doesn't say so, but it's obvious that the dying witness of Stephen powerfully affected and convicted him.

So that leaves a question: Should Stephen, who remained faithful and was murdered for his faith, be honored on the same level as the repentant thief on the cross who believed only minutes before he died?

"WHAT CAN YOU TELL US ABOUT REWARDS IN HEAVEN?"

"What about rewards?" the woman asked. "Did you receive yours while you were still there?" Before I could respond, she added, "And if you did, what were they?"

"On my brief visit to heaven, I didn't receive any reward. Except I was there. That was surely enough," I said. "But the time of rewards comes later."

I didn't want to go into a deep, theological lecture, so I tried to explain briefly, as I'm attempting to do here. God has rewards for our faithfulness. What we do for Him doesn't get us to heaven, but it does affect life in the new heaven and the new earth.

"Each will be rewarded according to their own labor" (1 Corinthians 3:8). Yes, but the rewards come at the Day (as used by Paul) or after the end of this world.

In 1 Corinthians 3:10–15, Paul writes about rewards by using the image of building a house. He starts by pointing out that Jesus is the foundation (verse 11). Then he adds, "If anyone builds on this foundation [faith in Jesus Christ], using gold, silver, costly stones, wood, hay or straw, their work will be shown for what it is, because the Day will bring it to the light. It will be revealed with fire, and the fire will test the quality of each person's work. If what has been built survives, the builder will receive a reward. If it is burned up, the builder will suffer loss but yet will be saved—even though only as one escaping through the flames" (verses 12–15).

There is a day of reckoning—of handing out punishment and bestowing rewards. Here again is the apostle's statement, "For we must all appear before the judgment seat of Christ, that everyone may receive what is due them for the things done while in the body, whether good or bad" (2 Corinthians 5:10).

The subject of rewards appears many times in the New Testament. In the Sermon on the Mount, Jesus talks about being persecuted for our faith and adds, "Rejoice and be glad, because great is your reward in heaven" (Matthew 5:12).

Jesus also gives two examples in Matthew 25. The first is the parable of the bags of gold given to three workers. They're called *talents*, and scholars say a talent was worth about twenty years of a day laborer's pay. Jesus rewards the first two. The third did nothing but hide his gold. Jesus says it was taken from him and given to the man who had started with five (see Matthew 5:14–30).

Immediately following that parable Jesus, referring to Himself, says, "When the Son of Man comes in his glory, and all the angels with him, he will sit on his glorious throne" (Matthew 25:31). He tells us that sheep (believers) will be on His right and be rewarded; the goats (unbelievers) will be on His left and He'll say to them, "Depart from me, you who are cursed, into the eternal life prepared for the devil and his angels" (verse 41).

———◆———

I don't know what form those rewards will take—but I know they'll be far, far greater than we can imagine. Our rewards depend on the goodness and power of God.

The rewards we gain in heaven aren't like the rewards we earn here on earth. We tend to think in material terms—mansions, jewels, prestige, and honor.

The Bible figuratively lists five crowns for believers:

1. A crown of righteousness for those who long for His appearing (2 Timothy 4:8).
2. An incorruptible crown for disciplined bodies and self-control (1 Corinthians 9:25–27).
3. A crown of life for those who patiently endure trials (James 1:12).
4. A crown of glory, according to 1 Peter 5:2–4, which is for godly leaders: "Be shepherds of God's flock, that is under your care, watching over them—not because you must, but because you are willing as God wants you to be; not pursuing dishonest

gain, but eager to serve, not lording it over those entrusted to you, but being examples to the flock. And when the Chief Shepherd appears, you will receive the crown of glory that will never fade away."

5. A crown of rejoicing, sometimes referred to as a soul winner's crown. Paul writes to the believers in Thessalonica, "For what is our hope, our joy, or the crown in which we will glory in the presence of our Lord Jesus when he comes? Is it not you? Indeed, you are our glory and joy" (1 Thessalonians 2:19–20).

To this, I add one of my favorite quotations from Charles Haddon Spurgeon: "There are no crown-wearers in heaven who were not cross-bearers here below."[1]

"WILL WE BE DISAPPOINTED WITH REWARDS?"

I can think of only one time when someone asked a question that truly shocked me. He stood and raised his hand. "Sir, will we be happy in heaven when we see people who received greater rewards than we do? Especially if we feel we've worked harder for the Lord?"

I wasn't sure if I should laugh or ignore it. But then, I assumed he was serious so I gave him my best answer: "First, in heaven, we'll be perfect. All sin—which includes jealousy and envy—will be gone. We'll never have an unkind or unloving thought toward anyone. Ever."

---

1   *The Westminster Collection of Christian Quotations*, Martin H. Manser, Compiler (Westminster John Knox Press, 2001).

"I know that, but, uh, well, people who serve God longer or more faithfully—"

This time, impulsively I interrupted him. "Doesn't our heavenly Father see and know all things? Doesn't He know the hearts and intentions of everything we do?"

"Well, yes..."

"Do you think Jesus could possibly do anything—anything—that was unfair or unjust?"

"Oh, no, of course not."

"Trust me in this: When you reach heaven, all vying, envying, and jealousy will be absolutely erased from your mind. You'll be so filled with joy and praise that worshiping the Lord will be your greatest focus."

He smiled then and sat down.

Chapter 26

Since Your Trip to Heaven, Do You Conduct Funerals Differently?

Funerals can be unique opportunities for ministry. Often people who wouldn't go to church or any spiritual event will attend out of respect or sympathy for the family or to honor the deceased.

The person responsible for leading the funeral service or the memorial service bears a great challenge to balance honoring the deceased, comforting the mourners, and challenging the living.

Funerals are the most time-consuming, emotionally invested, and meticulous ministry events I do. From the beginning of my ministry, performing that service has been of utmost importance. I fervently pray for God to help me do my job well.

That hasn't changed. To those present who are already followers of Jesus, the service is a celebration of life.

Since the release of the book and movie *90 Minutes in Heaven*, some mourners in attendance know my story, and so my presence is an encouragement to them. When I speak about heaven at the funeral, they know they're getting a first-person account. I can see the hope on their faces. The fact that those mourners came gives me another opportunity to show them how to come to Christ if they haven't already done so.

I still say most of the same things I did before; I read Scriptures as I did before the accident. But since 1989, I speak with greater conviction and passion.

One of the Bible verses I often quote are Jesus' own words from John 11:26: "I am the resurrection and the life. The one who believes in me will live, even though they die, and whoever lives by believing in me will never die."

My friend Reverend Bob Liechty used to say at funerals, "We often refer to earth as the land of the living. It really is the land of the dying. Heaven is the land of the living." I quote that frequently because I grasp that truth far more deeply than ever.

Before the accident, I had no doubts and believed. But since then, I feel like the Samaritans who heard the sinful woman's story after she spoke with Jesus. She met Him, heard Him, then ran back to her home and told everyone. "Many of the Samaritans from that town believed in him because of the woman's testimony" (John 4:39).

Then Jesus Himself came and spoke with them for two days. Then we read: "They said to the woman, 'We no longer believe just because of what you said; now we have heard for ourselves, and we know that this man really is the Savior of the World'" (verse 42).

That's the best way I know how to explain the difference. I was a believer, but after I returned, I could speak with stronger conviction. I had seen enough of heaven just being at the gates that I could speak out of the richness of personal experience.

There is, however, one thing I've added since coming back from heaven when I do funerals. I leave the platform, walk over to the head of the casket, and place my hand on it. "In a few moments this service will conclude," I say. "On behalf of the friends and family, I want to again convey my sincerest of thanks for your being here today. It means so much." I invite them to join us at the graveside committal service.

I pause, point toward the casket, and add, "I must tell you, she won't be there. We're taking this casket and her earth suit there for burial. But while we're doing that, she's more alive today in heaven than she ever was here on earth. As the apostle Paul declared, 'To be absent from the body is to be present with the Lord.' Your separation from her is real, but it won't last," I say gently.

Doing funerals and memorial services today has become, for me, richer and more meaningful. Since my own encounter with death, I can say, "Before, I believed; now, I *know*. My heart is joyful over the arrival of one of God's saints at the gates of glory."

What Do You Want
Your Legacy to Be?

Chapter 27

The Ripple Effect

Who doesn't want to see immediate results from our commitment and service to Jesus Christ? Often, God withholds those positive responses for years—or might even hold them until we get to heaven.

One of the great blessings of my life as a believer is the ripple effect. That is, I do something that helps another person to change—to turn to Christ, to grow, to overcome problems. If they remain faithful, they pass it on. Then the ripples go from one person to another.

Here's an example of what I mean. His name is Tom Cole and he's still alive. He came into my life when I was sixteen years old. He made himself available to gently lead me in making my personal reservation in heaven. And almost every day I thank God that he did. Over the years, we lost contact with each other, although I never forgot him.

More than forty-five years later, I rushed to the Mardel Christian Bookstore in Oklahoma City. My publisher had just released my book *Getting to Heaven* and Mardel graciously invited me to sign books for their customers. During that same week, I was conducting a series of meetings in Oklahoma—what we Baptists call revival meetings.

I arrived at the store exactly at the agreed-on time, and as I walked in, several people had already gathered at the table where the manager had piled my books.

Less than two feet inside the store, I was stopped by a tall man with salt-and-pepper hair and glasses. He thrust a copy of my book at me. "Could you sign my book, please."

Looking past him at the people in line I replied, "Yes, sir, I'd be honored to sign your book, but these nice people are already waiting in line. It wouldn't be fair to sign yours at the door and have them wait while I do that."

"I'm in a really big rush. Could you, please?"

"Of course. Would you like me to put your name in it? What is it?"

He looked down at the book, grinned, and said, "Tom Cole."

As I started to write his name, I stopped and stared into his eyes. "Tom?"

He nodded.

I embraced him and turned to my waiting line at the book signing table. "Hey, everybody, this is Tom Cole, the man who prayed with me to accept Christ more than forty years ago."

Applause rang out from the crowd.

"Tom, what brings you here today?"

"You and your book," he answered, grabbing me by the shoulders.

"Is it ever great to see you," I said. "I'd lost track of you when you went to the mission field. Where are you now?" Dr. Cole told me about his wife being a professor at Oklahoma Baptist

University, and his retirement as the director of missions for an Oklahoma Baptist Association. He beamed when he said that he was still playing an upright bass, but instead of playing for youth as he did when I knew him, he was a member of a bluegrass band.

"That's amazing, brother. I still remember your playing at youth fellowships at First Baptist Bossier. But most of all, I remember your praying with me in my living room on Fullilove Drive."

"I remember it, too. We don't forget moments like that. I was actually serious about being in a rush. I'm so sorry."

"I'm preaching tomorrow night near here," I said. "Do you think you might be able to come? I'd love to visit some more."

"Yes, I'd like that," he replied, and I gave him the church address. We embraced again, and clutching the autographed book, he raced out the door.

The next evening, I started my revival meetings. I had decided to share my testimony about coming to know Jesus at age sixteen. I had already tried to make the point that we're not here only for our salvation, but we're appointed to help others make heavenly reservations.

When I reached the place in my story where Tom Cole explained to me how to become a Christian, I paused and stepped forward. "Joe Socks, Mike Wood, and others met me at the gates of heaven. Tom Cole met me at the 'gate' to Mardel's Bookstore in Oklahoma City.

"And the man who gave me that answer forty-five years ago is here tonight." I gestured toward him. "Tom Cole! Stand up!"

People applauded.

Below is an excerpt from the book I signed for Tom Cole, *Getting to Heaven: Departing Instructions for Your Life Now.*

We need to be able to say, "I believe...."

It's that simple. I made the decision when I was young, and that decision changed my life. At that moment, I knew where I was headed.

I didn't live every moment from age sixteen until I was hit by a truck at age thirty-eight thinking about eternity. I tried to focus on living a life that honored the God I had promised to serve. In fact, I was actually on my way to church to lead a Bible study when the accident occurred. But I lived what most people could call a normal life. It wasn't perfect, but I wanted God to be my focus....

Heaven is real. I know because I've experienced that reality. Someday I will cross the final bridge, and I'll meet those same people again at the gate. And they'll be joined by others whom I have loved and lost for just a little while, others who have passed on since I was last there. They'll usher me into the presence of Jesus Christ. The words I yearn to hear Jesus say, are, "Well done, good and faithful servant."

I want everyone to be ready. I want everyone to cross that final bridge with the assurance of a reserved space in heaven....

When I sign my books, I write, "See you at the gate," above my signature. That's been the focus of my life in the years since my brief trip to heaven.

If you're searching, may you make the right choice. Whether you die by disease or accident won't be your decision. You can, however, choose to be ready.

If you haven't done so, please make your reservation. If you do make that decision, someday, I hope to meet *you* at the gate.[1]

———————

That's the ripple effect in action.

Jan, Barry, and Carmen obeyed God by coming to my house and inviting me to church. Even though many people living and deceased had influenced me to accept Jesus as Savior, they were only the first "ripples." Tom Cole was the second ripple by explaining the way to salvation. I've helped keep those ripples going for more than fifty years.

Someday I'll meet Tom again. It won't be in Oklahoma City, and the only book that will matter is the Lamb's Book of Life. His name is in it and so is mine.

And by God's grace, I'll be able to see that ripple effect going on and on.

Will you keep the ripple going?

---

1   Don Piper and Cecil Murphey, *Getting to Heaven: Departing Instructions for Your Life Now* (New York: Berkley Publishing Group) 2011, pages 305–306.

Chapter 28

You *Can* Tell Your Story

As Christians, each of us has a testimony to share. Our faithful lives prove we can live a joyful life that provides answers and comforts for every need.

If you were an unbeliever, wouldn't you want to know that a good life is possible? Or when you were an unbeliever, didn't you want to experience the inner peace and joy that God offers?

Telling your story—painful or pleasant—is crucial to bringing souls to Jesus. No one can legitimately argue with your words "Here's what happened to me." We know what happened to us the moment we said yes to salvation. *That's your testimony.*

My decision was to share my profound encounters at the gates of heaven and struggle for meaning after my return. In many ways my testimony would be unique and challenging for many.

But it's my firm conviction that I needed to share my story about coming to Jesus Christ—to share the good news. My primary purpose in writing this book is to urge you to share your story of coming to Christ.

Immediately, I can hear the responses:

- "But, Don, I didn't get run over by a truck."
- "I didn't stay in a hospital bed for thirteen months and endure three years of therapy to learn to walk again."
- "My story is so ordinary. No one is going to listen to a person share a mundane life of growing up in church, going to Sunday school every week, and being at services every time the church doors open."
- "I was never addicted to drugs or alcohol; I didn't live a life of crime or immorality; I've been free of agony, disasters, and decadence."
- "I wasn't beaten and abused. I lived a normal life with a normal, loving family."

Sometimes I hear, "I don't have that gift. I'm shy. I'm not good with words." And I understand that, so I ask, "How about the way you live away from church?"

Our Christian witness is about more than words. Our lifestyle also proclaims who we are. All too often I sense that Christians want someone else to do the "heavy lifting" of witnessing. God can and will use all of us, not just us hired hands—the ordained clergy.

Or we wrap ourselves inside a Christian bubble so that it's been years since we talked with an unbeliever about Christ in our lives. We're too busy talking to the redeemed. Fellowship with the saints is truly a blessing, but when we influence another lost soul for Christ, we can fellowship with them for all eternity.

Often I hear people say, "We're such a friendly church." I believe that, but then I ask, "Are you friendly with church visitors? Do you warmly welcome them? What about people who don't look or dress like you?"

Perhaps you've encountered what I call false unworthiness. "Oh, I'm just not worthy to share Jesus with others." If worthiness is the yardstick for being entitled to witness, none of us is qualified. Thank the Lord, we're never alone in this. It's up to us *and* the Holy Spirit.

God won't force us to share the gospel any more than He forces us to be saved. But someone or many someones led you to Jesus.

We need to consider our sphere of influence and what we can do to point them to Jesus. We start with family and friends, and we don't stop there. Workplace, clubs, school, neighborhood, our daily commutes, our shopping locations, the dry cleaners, and church outreach opportunities. In short, anywhere and every-where we go.

In seminary, our class studied the original Greek language of the New Testament. One of the portions that has stayed with me, Matthew 28:19–20, has been translated as: "Therefore, go and make disciples of all nations, baptizing them in the name of the Father, the Son and the Holy Spirit, and teaching them to obey everything that I have commanded you. And surely, I am with you always, to the very end of the age."

The Greek word for *go* in the Great Commission means *as you go*. "As you go and make disciples" is the intent of Jesus' words. It's what we're commanded to do. Jesus implies that we share our faith as part of our daily lives.

Sharing Jesus offers us a lifetime of joy and opportunity. We can have complete confidence in what we do, because we're not re-sponsible for the results.

A verse that we need to bear in mind comes from Peter, who

admonishes, "Always be prepared to give an answer to everyone who asks you to give the reason for the hope that you have. But do this with gentleness and respect" (1 Peter 3:15).

In giving answers (bearing witness), we don't need to exaggerate our experience or make it sound more dramatic. It's *His* story we're trying to impart, but we normally start with our story of what the Lord has done in our lives.

For example, I was a national sales manager at a CBS television affiliate station for several years before my ministry days. I sent my sales staff out and encouraged them, "Don't just pitch the client; ask for the order!"

Like the salespeople, we don't always get the response we want. That's all right. Our role is to make the offer; the Holy Spirit is the one who convicts and draws them to Himself.

Of course, we may not receive a positive response immediately, or even in our lifetime. We can't allow that to discourage us. We do what Jesus commanded: "As you go..."

After my recovery from the accident, Pastor Dick Onarecker sat across from me at one of our regular lunches. I told him how grateful my family and friends were for his obedience in climbing into a demolished car and praying over my dead body.

He began to weep. "Anyone would have done it," Dick said. "If we see a child drifting toward a busy street, we react. We want to save them. That's what I did on the bridge that morning."

He looked around. "Here we are in a Denny's restaurant and there are probably souls in this place who are dying and going to hell without Christ. Praying for you in that car reminded me: We all have much work to do. The world is lost and we have to tell them about Jesus."

Dick was right: We all have much work to do.

Jesus said the two greatest commands are to love God with our total being and to love our neighbors as ourselves (see Matthew 22:37–39). To love others means to want the best for them. What's a better offering than joyful peace with God and assurance of eternal life?

No two lives are the same. For example, Jesus talked to a woman at a well who had had five husbands and was living with a sixth man (see John 4).

A ruler turned from Jesus because he wasn't willing to give up his possessions to help the poor and needy. And yet, he had just finished saying that he had kept all the commandments "since I was a boy" (Luke 18:21). We'd call him self-righteous—outwardly religious but inwardly empty.

That's only two examples—an obviously sinful woman and an ethical, lawful man. Both needed to know salvation through Jesus Christ. The woman at the well turned to Him. Of the ethical man, Luke records, "And when he heard [Jesus' words], he became very sad, because he was wealthy" (Luke 18:23).

Their dissimilar backgrounds weren't the issue. Both needed something more in life, and Jesus loved them equally. He directed His message to meet their situations and allowed them to make their life choices.

As you've already read, at age sixteen, I came to know Jesus through the words and deeds of the people God nudged to come and visit me. None of them saw themselves as doing anything special for God. They showed me Jesus by the way they lived—their friendliness and eagerness to accept me. They cared about me, and because they cared, they taught me how to know Jesus. Our task is to faithfully present our lives as living witnesses.

Bringing souls to a saving knowledge of Christ often involves baiting a lot of hooks. When I was a kid, my dad, Master Sergeant Ralph Piper, was often overseas on active duty. How my brothers and I loved it when he would come home and spend time with us!

One of our favorite activities to do with him was fishing. We used fishing rods and sometimes mechanisms called yo-yos, which were tied to low-hanging trees and spring-loaded. Our favorite fishing method was using trotlines. We strung a long, strong fishing line across open water, sometimes even a channel. Then we tied the ends of the main line to trees or stumps. At various intervals from the main line we dropped short, smaller fishing lines to hang down into the water with baited hooks. In the afternoon, we changed the sizes of the hooks, the kinds of bait, and locations several times. *The objective never changed: We wanted to catch fish.* And we caught a lot on those trotlines.

All through the night we ventured out in a boat to "run the trotlines." As we approached each hanging hook, we knew a fish was on the line because it thrashed in the water.

When sharing Jesus with lost people, we need to set a lot of hooks, use different baits (winning techniques), and fish in different locations.

Likewise, a farmer who expects to successfully bring in a harvest has to keep planting seed. It's an ongoing process until the crops are fully harvested. Jesus needs workers in all fields!

Recently, I sat in a restaurant with a pastor and his staff in Southern California. Our table was serviced by a cordial hard-working young lady. Her name tag read Tayllor.

She took our beverage orders. When she returned with our drinks, the pastor said, "Tayllor, we're about to pray for our meal, do you have anything on your heart that we can pray for?"

She acted a little flustered, then quietly offered several things that she wanted us to pray for. All of us, including Tayllor, prayed together. Before the meal was over, I signed a copy of *90 Minutes in Heaven* to Tayllor and she promised to come to church the next Sunday.

It was that simple.

But it's not always that simple. I met a man in Houston who prayed for his best friend's son for twenty-one years before that young man trusted Jesus.

Tommy Freeman is another example. A dear friend of many and a great influence on my early days of youth ministry, he used to get excited when he was going to fly somewhere. He knew that for the duration of the flight, he would be in a metal tube soaring at forty thousand feet for at least a couple of hours. Whenever possible, Tommy chose the center seat so he could tell others about Jesus. And tell them he did.

We have to set a lot of hooks, and use a lot of bait. Sometimes we catch fish, and sometimes we're just the seed planters. My father planted peach trees in the winter of his life. He never ate from those trees. But his grandchildren did.

———◆———

As you can see, there are as many approaches, opportunities, and situations as there are people. Availability and sensitivity are crucial. We also need to remind ourselves that the Holy Spirit is in control. We do what we can; the Spirit does the rest.

In 1986, my dear friend David Gentiles and I held the very first youth camp at Camp Bethany, which straddles the Louisiana-Texas border near Shreveport. After much planning, we felt confident that the Lord would bless our youth camp.

All week long, the Spirit was moving among our kids. Each night before retiring, the staff gathered for an assessment and planning session. All on our staff agreed that on Thursday night, the night before the camp concluded, we'd offer an invitation for young people to come forward and share their decisions for Jesus at a celebratory worship service.

For Wednesday night, we scheduled a concert with a Christian contemporary band from South Louisiana. The room was packed and the band was amazing.

As the concert concluded, the lead singer stepped up to the mic and said, "You know, I feel the Spirit moving tonight in a special way. We're going to sing a special song now. If you feel like coming to the front for prayer, or if you want to make a decision to follow Jesus, just come as we sing. Be obedient."

They began to play. Our staff looked at David and me, as if to ask, *What do we do now?* The invitation we had planned wasn't until the following night. The counselors who were to greet the kids weren't yet ready.

The band continued to play and the teens streamed down the aisles for nearly an hour. The band members were clearly joyful because of the response.

Frankly, David and I and our staff were miffed that the band members didn't ask us if they could offer an invitation. They hadn't been at the camp and hadn't known what we had planned. But none of us said anything to the band after the concert.

The following night's planned invitation was still wonderful, but it wasn't what we had anticipated.

Years later, the leader of that band became the pastor of a church in Baton Rouge. I reminded him of the story of Camp Bethany and how taken aback we were by the "presumptuousness" of his altar call.

He smiled and said, "What you don't know is that our band prayed before that concert. We'd been discouraged, not seeing any response to what we were trying to do. After prayer, we decided that if we didn't see some confirmation that we were in the center of God's will, we'd go back to Baton Rouge and disband. That night we knew we were exactly where God wanted us to be. When I felt the Spirit move me to offer an invitation, I knew it was of God."

"And it was," I said.

Then I apologized for our attitude. We had a plan; God had a better one. New names were written down in glory on Wednesday, and Thursday.

We may not live to see the results of our labors for Jesus. But those folks who directly experienced our spiritual influence in their lives will meet us someday at the gates of heaven.

Whenever I extend an altar call or invitation at the conclusion of a sermon, I'm reminded that the response to the message is God's work. Paul expresses this when he writes about the work of God's servants: "What, after all, is Apollos? And who is Paul? Only servants, through whom you came to believe—as the Lord has assigned to each of us his task. I planted the seed, Apollos watered it, but God has been making it grow" (1 Corinthians 3:5–6).

Then we wait until we get to heaven to experience the joy of our efforts. At the gates of heaven I met those who helped me get there, and they got to celebrate the eternal reality of their investment in my salvation. While still on earth, some of them had no idea how effective their words and actions were in my life.

On earth, we plant seeds, and perhaps someone else waters, and the harvest is witnessed by others. Results aren't our responsibility.

Chapter 29

What Is in Your Hand?

God commissioned Moses to confront the ruler of Egypt and to lead the people of Israel out of slavery. Then, Moses, aware of his own weakness and probably in fear, asked, "What if they don't believe me?" (Exodus 4:1).

God shifted Moses' attention away from himself by asking, "What is in your hand?" (verse 2).

Moses said it was a staff (a shepherd's rod), and "the LORD said, 'Throw it on the ground.' Moses threw it on the ground and it became a snake, and [Moses] ran from it" (verse 3).

The lesson for Moses—and for us today—is that we worry about how we're going to do something, as if to take total responsibility for accomplishing God's will.

The Lord showed Moses that He was in the business of using the ordinary to do the extraordinary.

I want to tell you how God used the ordinary to do His will in my life and in the lives of others.

One such time was a Sunday in November 2017. I woke that morning and got dressed to attend services at my home church,

First Baptist of Pasadena, Texas. I wasn't feeling well and wasn't scheduled to preach anywhere that morning. I seriously considered resting at home and watching the service streaming on the Internet.

As service time grew closer, I decided to go anyway. Eva and I drove to church, walked in the north entrance, and were immediately ambushed, not three steps inside the door.

A nice young lady named Jennifer said, "I came to see you today. I want you to meet my father, Michael Peavy, who's dying of cancer." She explained that she had seen my book *Heaven Is Real* in a thrift shop and bought it for a dollar. After reading it, she purchased audio books of *Heaven Is Real* and *90 Minutes in Heaven* so that her dad could listen to them. His cancer was so advanced, he could no longer hold a book.

She had driven from Oklahoma City to Houston to bring her terminally ill father to church. Michael lived on the other side of Houston, probably a forty-five-minute drive on a good-traffic day.

"Where is he?"

"Sitting in the back pew."

I went to him and introduced myself. It was nearly time for the worship service to begin, so I suggested we sit in the lobby.

Despite his being obviously ill and weak, he got up, and slowly walked with me. Jennifer came out with us and sat nearby. While we talked, she prayed silently as she balanced her two-year-old daughter on her hip.

By his own admission, Michael was an agnostic or borderline atheist and yet interested in spiritual things. As we talked, I thought, *Impending death can be a great motivator for confronting eternity.*

Michael had a barrage of questions. I did my best to answer.

We were so involved that the service concluded while we were still talking in the church commons.

By then, I could see that Michael had exhausted his strength, and yet I sensed he was open to the Holy Spirit. "Can I come visit you at your home?" I asked.

"Yes, but my daughter is moving me to hospice in Oklahoma City at the end of the week."

"How about Tuesday?"

Michael looked stunned that I would actually visit his home.

We set the time and he gave me his address.

On my way home from church, I read an e-mail that Jennifer had sent me before the service began but I hadn't had a chance to see: "My father says there is no heaven. The Bible says there is. Please pray for his salvation. He hasn't long to live."

I prayed passionately for Michael's salvation and our upcoming meeting. However, before that meeting could take place, Jennifer called me from Michael's apartment in Houston, where she was packing bags for his final earthly trip. "Dad wants to share something with you, Pastor Piper." She handed him the phone.

In a weak but joyful voice, Michael Peavy told me that minutes earlier, he and his daughter had prayed together as he gave his heart to Jesus and made his reservation in heaven.

"Now I'll be able to see you there," I said.

I kept my appointment on Tuesday. What I assumed would be an hour-long meeting turned into four hours. It wasn't easy to say good-bye to someone who knew me well because he had recently listened to two of my books.

He went to be with Jesus only a few days later.

Not only did I rejoice in Michael's salvation, but it reminded me that the Holy Spirit can use many ways to get to open hearts.

If you had asked Jennifer what was in her hand, she could have said, "Only a book." But that was the beginning of God's wonderful miracle. One book of mine—discovered in a thrift store—influenced Jennifer to take action for the salvation of her dying father.

Or think about this. When I was in elementary school, a member of Gideon International distributed free Bibles to students (it's no longer allowed in most public schools). It was the first Bible that I ever owned. Other loving people presented me with Bibles as I grew older. I devoured them!

How many people have come to Christ simply through someone volunteering to give away Bibles to children? In this life, we'll never know.

Or I can go back in my life and think of the people who looked at what was in their hands—what they had and what they could do.

My next-door neighbor invited me to church when I was nine years old and took me there in a station wagon loaded with neighborhood kids. My grandmother took me to church whenever I visited her. Jan, Carmen, and Barry came to my house and invited me to church when I was sixteen. Sue and Nellie and Charlie and J. R. and Hattie and Joe Socks and Charlotte taught me how to live and pray and believe.

I often remind myself that no matter what we have in our hands, if we use what we have, God honors that. All those people from my childhood gave what they had. It all counts: everything we do to point others to Jesus.

In Romans 10:14, the apostle Paul wrote to the laypeople of Rome—and it applies to us all as well: "How, then, can they call on the one they have not believed in? And how can they believe in the one of whom they have not heard? And how can they hear without someone preaching to them?"

If you're a follower of Jesus Christ, this is about you. The lost need to hear from you. Have you considered that you may be the only real preacher of the gospel others will hear?

Jennifer could tell you that the Christian books she bought and her prayers culminated when she put her dying father in her car and brought him to church. Now she knows he is in heaven and has the awesome peace of knowing that her witness helped him get there. Anything that I did was simply a cog in the wheel of Michael's salvation.

———◆———

What is in *your* hand? Consider that seriously.

What do I have in my mind right now? A passion to see everyone come to know Jesus Christ. When I preach, I never assume that everyone in the audience is already a believer. Hearing me speak that day might be that individual's only encounter with Christ. Even in the Bible, Jesus often meets a person only once. At least, we have no biblical record of their meeting again on earth.

Do you know Him? If you don't know Jesus, right now is a splendid time to ask Him into your heart. My sincere prayer is that many readers of this book will come to love my family and friends of faith who gathered to meet me at the gates of heaven. Even more, I deeply hope and pray that you'll be greeting your own host of followers of Jesus at the gates of heaven someday, because *you* helped them get there! Starting now!

If you're already a believer and you're still alive today, what do you suppose that means? My unqualified conviction is that we're still *here* to help everyone else get *there*.

At the age of twelve, Jesus amazed the religious leaders and teachers of the law. When His parents interrupted Him, saying they were worried about Him, He answered, "Did you not know that I must be about My Father's business" (Luke 2:49 NKJV).

So must we!

Chapter 30

"You Tell Him"

At Barksdale Baptist in Bossier City, I experienced my first leadership role in youth ministry. My friend Tommy Freeman saw that I had the gift of youth leadership and volunteered me to lead our youth. I loved it right away. Discipleship Weekend was one of our annual events in youth ministry. We divided the kids by gender and age and spent a weekend in a church member's home. The host homes and other volunteers provided food and a safe place. Very little sleep took place. We built fun times into the schedule as well as team-building concepts. Many kids invited their friends for the weekend. Most important, talented adults led the young people into a closer walk with Jesus.

One of the highlights of the weekend was that each group participated in a service project for the church or community. An elderly person's home or yard might be cleaned for them. Maybe a homeless shelter had food prepared and served by the youth.

Before concluding the Discipleship Weekend on Sunday evening with a service of songs, testimonies, and decision time, we gathered in a smaller room away from the church auditorium.

That allowed kids who might not be willing to speak before the whole church an opportunity to share with their peers. Some of the best and most meaningful testimonies came out of these pre-service sharing sessions.

It was amazing to observe the incredible changes the kids and adults underwent since their initial meeting together on Friday night. Many of them hadn't known each other nor what to expect.

I led one testimony pre-service, which began with prayer and silly stories of pranks that had taken place in each home, causing a lot of laughter. Then the tone of our testimony time became serious. Some kids emotionally shared decisions that they had made for salvation, for a deeper walk with Jesus, and new concerns for others.

That evening, an elderly woman sat in the middle of the group. I hadn't remembered her signing up for the weekend as a host home or helper. Yet she sat in rapt attention. A few times she dabbed tears from her eyes. More than once, her face beamed with joy. Suddenly she stood and cleared her throat. She said her name was Mrs. Reynolds. "I came to church this afternoon to attend a ladies' meeting. I thought that they had changed rooms because they usually meet in here. I sat down. Then all of you arrived and I was too embarrassed to get up and leave.

"All along I kept thinking, *I'm in the wrong meeting*. But the longer I sat here, the more I realized I wasn't in the wrong meeting. This is the right meeting for me 'cause I couldn't be prouder of my church for doing something like this. I couldn't be prouder of what God is doing with you—our young people. But most of all, I see the friends that you invited to church so that they could know Jesus."

Tears came to her eyes and she paused before she added, "I've got friends, too. And I haven't asked them to come to church."

She leaned on her walker and headed for the door. Then Mrs. Reynolds stopped and exclaimed, "There's just enough time before tonight's service to invite them, and I'm going to do that right now! Pray for me!"

After she left, the room became absolutely silent. Then a boy about fifteen years old stood. "I'm a visitor. My friend Jacob invited me. This has been one of the best things I've ever been to. Y'all have been so nice to me and I've learned so much. One lesson is that a lot of people don't know about Jesus. I haven't known him for too long myself, but I found him last night and now I'm sure I'm going to heaven."

Kids applauded all over the room.

"I've got a little brother, Ben. We don't always get along too well. But he is my brother and I love him." He seemed unaware that tears had started sliding down his cheeks. "I sure don't want to go to heaven without him. I'm sorry and I hate to miss tonight's service. I hope y'all won't be upset with me but I gotta go tell Ben about Jesus right away."

Sobs erupted from all over the room as other teens started crying. When he was in control of his emotions, he said, "Thanks again for everything. Pray for Ben. I gotta go." And he ran out.

Do you know a Ben?

———

When I was on the staff of Airline Baptist, I had a marvelous group of teenagers in my youth group. But I also had the support of some caring parents as well. I began my duties not long before the summer season, so I had little time to plan a complete youth camp. In youth ministry circles, that usually means taking your youth to a pre-planned camp. I chose to have summer camp on the campus of Louisiana College in Pineville, Louisiana, and we called the event Kaleidoscope.

Our church was growing rapidly, and our youth group was exploding. Enrollment for the camp was fast. When I looked at the list of attendees, I felt so proud that our church kids had invited their friends to be with us.

We had a tremendous experience that year at Kaleidoscope. One of the nightly preaching services focused on sharing our faith with the unsaved.

A gaggle of our guys seemed particularly moved. They sought me out afterward and shared that they didn't believe that one of their buddies, Trey, had ever trusted Jesus as Savior. I had suspected as much when I talked to him earlier in the week.

One afternoon, some of Trey's friends sneaked into the school auditorium to find me. They said they thought Trey was close to making a decision for Christ and asked if I would come and talk to him.

For guys in their mid to late teens, that was unusually perceptive. They were quite emotional about it. My immediate thought was to drop what I was doing and make tracks to find Trey. Just then, I felt the tugging of the Spirit in my own heart. I looked them all straight in the eyes and said, "No, he's your friend. You invited him. You tell him how to know Jesus."

"But we don't know what to say. We don't want to mess this up. Trey means a lot to us," they argued.

"That's exactly why I want you to talk to him. You do know what to say. Some of you have been going to church since you were babies. Now get out of here."

They left, and I immediately launched into prayer for them.

Later, just before the evening service, I was in the auditorium. The lobby doors opened and several kids came screaming down the aisles, out of breath, and trying to speak between tears of joy. I finally was able to make out their ecstatic words: "Trey...just... got...saved!"

Trey's friends had led him to Christ, not youth pastor Don Piper. His buddies did, who would be his friends before and after Kaleidoscope. They loved him enough to do whatever it took to see that they spent eternity with Trey. I wouldn't have taken that joy away from them at any price. Even more, never again could they say, "But I can't do this. I don't know how."

Wouldn't it be tremendous if we could get that excited about those with whom we come into contact coming to Jesus? That we would want to scream and weep for all the world to hear, "Trey just got saved!"

We all know how. We just need to open our mouths and speak of the One we love.

Chapter 31

Who Will Be in Heaven Because of You?

What do you want your legacy to be? I can give you a pre-wreck answer and a post-wreck answer to this question. It may sound like the same answer, but it's not.

My initial response is: Why would anyone possibly want to know what my legacy is to be? I don't think about it. Why should I? I won't be around to enjoy it.

But I confess, that reply is tinged with hypocrisy considering how much emphasis I've placed in this book on telling your own story—your conversion testimony.

I've lost count of the times I've stood before crowds and urged each person present: "You need to turn your test into a testimony; your pain into a purpose. Turn your mess into a message. Make your tragedy into a triumph. Move from bitter to better." I've testified before thousands that I've been knocked down but not knocked out; I have been beaten up but not beaten. After my accident, many saw me as a victim. I decided to become a victor. Even though there may be thousands in the audience, it's always personal: one soul at a time. Salvation is the most personal decision of all time.

On the morning of January 18, 1989, I was a pastor on my way to church. At South Park Church, I served as a pastor for education ministry and youth ministry. Before that I'd been in the broadcasting industry professionally for eleven years. I achieved some recognition for becoming the youngest national sales manager for a network TV affiliate in history.

If you had knocked on my door at Trinity Pines Conference Center on the evening of January 17, 1989, and asked, "What do you want your legacy to be?" likely, I would have answered, "To be a faithful servant of God, a good son, a good father, a good husband, a patriot."

So post-wreck, how would I answer? I've had a lot of time to think about it in a hospital bed, during therapy for nearly three years, and because I get asked by members of my audiences.

I hope this doesn't sound boastful, but trying to answer the legacy question has brought this to the surface. I think about being born in an army hospital when my mother was nineteen years old and a thousand miles from her home. Or about going to first grade wearing a shirt my mother made from a flour sack and a coat she fashioned from corduroy. I think about the Army moving us every couple of years and sending my dad to Korea and Vietnam.

I think about being hurt as a young boy in ways that I have shared with very few people. It's a legacy of joy and pain, being loved, and the deep sacrifice from those who loved me. These things affected me in profound ways. I come from sturdy stock. I do have an extraordinarily high threshold for pain of all types; I believe that has been one of my greatest assets and greatest burdens. I have thanked God continuously that the truck hit *me* and no one else. I would never want what happened to me to happen to someone else.

People say I'm a good listener and that I'm willing to take time with them. Forming a nonprofit ministry to others in need has been one of my greatest joys. I felt privileged to be able to minister to the Navajos in New Mexico and the Sioux in Montana. Supporting Christian camps for adults and children in need, Teen Challenge, African ministries, crisis pregnancy centers, and inner-city shelters has provided some of the awesome adventures God has placed in front of me. Counseling in juvenile detention facilities and speaking in prisons all over the country are humbling and immensely rewarding experiences.

Many times I've held the hands of critically ill people and talked to them about heaven as they were about to depart this life. I cherish the opportunities to visit with kids and adults wearing external fixators who want to be with someone who understands what it is like to endure such monstrosities.

I've prayerfully cowritten five books, and a movie has been made about my life. Those'll be around after I'm gone.

Millions of miles and faces are a legacy. Sometimes when I get quiet late at night back at the hotel I can still see them—hurting, curious, lonely, seeking, hopeful. I've seen a million smiles and two million tears.

Years ago when I was just a kid myself, I was leading a youth camp at Barksdale Baptist Church. The subject came up of what we wanted our legacies to be. I'm not certain we were old enough to know what a legacy was. But as most of the group floundered around, I thought I'd take a stab at it.

I cleared my throat and said, "When I'm gone, I want people to say, 'He made a difference in my life.'"

Those words came from a place that I had never really explored. Forty years later I'd enlarge that to say, "And I want to make known the love of Jesus Christ to as many people as I can while I can."

Who will be in heaven because of you?

Questions for Further Reflection

CHAPTER 1
I DIED AND ENTERED HEAVEN

- Do you have difficulty believing someone could die, go to heaven, and return to life on earth? If so, why?
- Why do you think Don waited two years before telling those closest to him about his heavenly experience?
- Don's wife said that he was different after he returned from heaven. How do you think a visit to heaven would change a person's life? How would it change *your* life?
- Dick Onarecker prayed for Don although he was dead. Because of his prayers, Don came back to life. Have you ever hesitated to pray for something, even when you sensed God's nudging? What keeps you from praying "big prayers"?
- Don tells his audiences that they don't have to be afraid of death. How does knowing that your earthly days are numbered affect the way you live your life, and how might that

impact your neighbors, your coworkers, your friends and family, your city, your country, and the world?

- "Heaven is a blissful buffet for our senses," Don writes. What do you look forward to most on the buffet? Why?

CHAPTER 2
MY CALLING

- Why is heaven such a popular topic?
- What do you believe is the driving force behind Don's desire to tell people about heaven?
- Don said his life today is filled with magnificent joy and profound pain. How is it possible for joy and pain to coexist?
- How does having knowledge of heaven give people a sense of hope?
- From what you've learned through personal Bible study or the teaching of others, what do you know to be true about heaven?
- Imagine having an experience like Don describes. How do you think that would affect your life?
- How would Jesus become more real to a person after having an experience like Don's?
- Why would a heavenly experience create a compulsion to reach out to others and tell them about Jesus Christ?
- How could an NDE or a glimpse of heaven remove someone's fear of death?
- What kind of fears do you have about death?

CHAPTER 3
AWE AND WONDER

- Don connects many Scripture verses with his heavenly experience. How do they help you understand heaven in a better way?
- Imagine the rejoicing that takes place in heaven when someone makes a reservation to go there. How do you envision such an event in *your* life?
- Don said the people he met in heaven were perfect and ageless. What's your emotional response to that?

Ponder Don's question: *"Why did God allow me a glimpse of heaven and then take that away from me?"* How would you answer it?

CHAPTER 4
MY INFLUENCERS

- This chapter starts with "None of those in my welcoming committee had been perfect humans." How does that make you feel? Does it give you hope?
- Don sees himself as a by-product of his welcoming committee's faith and faithfulness. How does that statement affect you?
- "I'm not certain that asking questions is ever necessary in heaven," Don wrote. Why won't our questions matter?
- Whom would you expect to be in your greeting committee when you reach heaven?
- What is a salvation experience, and from what are you saved?

CHAPTER 5
JAN COWART

- How comfortable are you about inviting people to church or telling someone about Jesus?
- Don said that it took him a few months to grasp the concept that we are *in* the world but not *of* the world. What does that phrase mean to you?
- If your friends had questions about Jesus or the Bible, would you be able to answer them, like Jan Cowart did for Don? If not, what would you do?
- Name two or three individuals who pointed you to the Savior. In what way did they help you?
- Whom have *you* encouraged to walk more closely with Jesus Christ?

CHAPTER 6
MIKE WOOD

- Mike had so many fine personal traits and enormous potential, the world could easily ask, "Why did Mike need Jesus?" How would you answer that question?
- Mike didn't apologize for his faith. What causes people to speak with such confidence and self-assurance?
- Although Mike and Don Piper didn't seem to have much in common, Mike's actions made an indelible impression on Don. If you were to die today, what would people say about you?
- Rather than ignoring Don (or bullying him) because he was different, Mike encouraged him. What are some of the ways

he did that, and how can you put something similar into practice right now?

- People react to the death of loved ones in various ways. How could their grieving process be different if they knew what Don knows of heaven?

CHAPTER 7
CHARLIE DINGMAN

- Why do you think Charlie Dingman was one of those who greeted Don Piper?
- One of Charlie's greatest joys was seeing attendance at his church grow because of his prayers. What joys have you experienced as a result of your prayers?
- Charlie inspired Don by praying for the humanly impossible. What is a humanly impossible request you have? Do you believe God is able to answer it?
- Whom does Charlie Dingman represent in your life?
- What one ongoing action will you commit to that encourages others to serve the Lord? (It could be as simple as visiting them or sending cards, e-mails, or texts to those you miss seeing at church.)

CHAPTER 8
SUE BELLE MCREA GUYTON

- How does showing love for family members and others make a difference in the lives of those watching us?
- What actions show people that you love them and genuinely care for them?

- Rather than judging people or looking down on them because of their unwise choices, what are loving ways to help them get back on the right path?
- Sue made it clear to Don that she was always there for him. What would it take for you to become a person like that?
- If you knew something that could seriously help another, to what lengths would you go to share it?

CHAPTER 9
GRANDMA NELLIE PIPER

- What does it mean to see Jesus in someone?
- What are ways to quietly prepare someone to follow Jesus?
- What does "being content whatever the circumstances" mean to you?
- How does being a praying person show up in the way you live, and how does it affect others?
- What would you like printed on your grave marker?

CHAPTER 10
JOE SOCKS

- What made Don believe Papa was in heaven?
- Don describes his grandfather as the "swellest" person he has ever known. If there's someone in your life you could say that about, what makes them "swell"?
- Why do you think Papa was the first person Don saw when he arrived?
- Don said he knew Papa was in heaven, even though some other Christians might not have thought so. What does a per-

son who "makes it to heaven" look like? What does God see that others might not?

- How can Don be so certain that he'll never see Papa cry again?

CHAPTER 11
J. R. AND HATTIE MANN

- How can a person know someone loves them, even though the words aren't spoken?
- What spiritual influence did your family impart to you? What spiritual influence are you imparting to your family?
- Don talks about his great-grandparents' faithfulness. In what way did that speak to him?
- In heaven, Don's great-grandmother wasn't stooped over from osteoporosis. She also had her own beautiful teeth. What kind of healing and renewal do you look forward to in heaven?
- Imagine that God has a front porch. What does it look like?

CHAPTER 12
CHARLOTTE JAYNES

- What are some of the things Don remembered about Miss Jaynes? How were they instrumental in preparing him for heaven?
- When Don was nearing graduation, Miss Jaynes told him that it was important to be firmly grounded in his faith. What advice would you give to a student?
- Miss Jaynes taught Don about effective communication. The most important thing he learned from her is that even before you've said your first word, the audience has already begun

to form an opinion about you. What does that mean for you?

- Don said that Miss Jaynes's support after he became a believer sustained him. Why does a believer need support?

- If you were to "give a speech" to those who have positively and greatly influenced your life, what would that speech say?

CHAPTER 13
WHO WILL MEET HIM?

- What does Don mean by "temporary separation" when referring to someone who just died?

- How do the words "temporary separation" encourage you?

- What do you think of Don's answer to the woman about who would greet her son at the gate? Do you agree?

- How could Don be so certain of his answer?

- How do you feel about being assured that no one is ever alone in heaven?

CHAPTER 14
THE WHY QUESTIONS

- Ponder Don's why questions. How would you answer them?

- What is a similar question you've asked? Did you ever receive an answer that worked for you?

- How would changing your *why* questions to *what* questions make a difference in your life?

- Why are people skeptical of Don's story?

- What's your response to Don's invitation to meet him at the gate?

CHAPTER 15
WHY DID GOD TAKE MY LOVED ONE?

- Have you asked, "Why did God take my loved one?" If so, what kinds of answers have you received?
- Why is there such pain when a loved one dies?
- After a loved one's death, how can you use your powerful emotions to glorify God?
- How does knowing that your loved one was on loan from God or that God is in control encourage you?
- What do you think about Don's interesting perspective on why Jesus wept at Lazarus' tomb?

CHAPTER 16
WHAT ABOUT THOSE WHO *DIDN'T* MEET YOU AT THE GATES?

- Think about your life and the people you expect to greet you the moment you enter into heaven.
- What will it be like to see Jesus face-to-face?

CHAPTER 17
WHY DIDN'T YOU SEE JESUS?

- Even though Don didn't see Jesus, how was His presence in heaven utterly unmistakable?
- How would you explain the significance and meaning of the Lamb of God?
- What does it mean to bask in Jesus' glory? Is that something we can do on earth, or can it be done only in heaven?

- Why would seeing a glimpse of the Savior cause Don to lose all will to live?

CHAPTER 18
THE MOST COMMON QUESTIONS I'M ASKED

- Who is someone you're curious about whether they're in heaven, and why?
- Don said it's hard to imagine experiencing complete bliss. Try imagining it. What would it feel like for you?
- Do you agree or disagree with Don's statement that if we knew who wasn't there, it wouldn't be heaven? Why?
- Why would people want to know whether their loved ones in heaven can see them?
- How are you comforted by knowing how quickly Christians arrive at the gates of heaven after they die?

CHAPTER 19
WHY DOESN'T GOD TAKE US TO HEAVEN THE MOMENT WE ACCEPT CHRIST?

- What would you have missed out on if you had been taken to heaven the moment you received Christ?
- What would others have missed out on if you had been taken to heaven the moment you received Christ?
- How has your life changed since receiving Christ?
- What does it mean to be saved to serve?
- What is your purpose?

CHAPTER 20
WHAT HAPPENS TO OUR BODIES IN HEAVEN?

- How did you think aging affected Adam and Eve after their banishment from Eden?
- How could one bad choice affect generations to come?
- What comes to mind when you think about living forever in a healthy, whole, and ageless body?
- Do you think living forever will seem like forever?
- How do you understand our heavenly bodies will differ from our earthly bodies?
- How are our bodies like seeds?
- What do you think Paul means by "Flesh and blood cannot inherit the kingdom of God"?
- How did the resurrection of Jesus change the course of history?
- Why didn't people recognize Jesus after the resurrection?

CHAPTER 21
DO WE BECOME ANGELS IN HEAVEN?

- Why do you think people talk about God needing another angel in heaven?
- Why would anyone think those who enter heaven become angels?
- How does the thought of angels comfort people?
- What does it mean to be "like the angels"?
- What do you understand the purpose of angels to be?

CHAPTER 22
WHEN BABIES DIE, DO THEY GO TO HEAVEN?

- Have you ever faced the question about babies going to heaven? Does Don's answer help?
- What do you believe happens to babies and young children after they die? Did Don's answer make you think differently?
- How does God's grace affect the situation?
- What new thought did you take away from the Scriptures that Don used?
- Why doesn't God provide answers to such questions as what happens to babies who die?

CHAPTER 23
A PERSONAL RESPONSE ABOUT BABIES WHO DIE

- How could Don's answer comfort and assure a person who has lost an unborn child?
- Why do stages of life happen only on earth?
- What does 2 Samuel 12:21 mean to you? Does Don's explanation of it encourage you? Why?
- How does the age of accountability factor into a child's being in heaven?
- Why didn't Don see any babies or children in heaven? Does that mean they're not there?

CHAPTER 24
WILL THERE BE PETS IN HEAVEN?

- Don said that the most emotional question he gets asked is about pets in heaven. Why is that?
- Why does the Bible depict dogs differently from the way we see them today?
- Why is it important to think about the culture when reading the Bible?
- Do you think you'll need pets in heaven to be happy?
- What does it mean to you that we'll have absolutely no unfulfilled needs in heaven?

CHAPTER 25
REWARDS IN HEAVEN

- How would you describe a life of faithfulness?
- How does God reward our faithfulness while we're still alive on earth?
- How do you believe God will reward your faithfulness once you're in heaven?
- Why isn't being with Jesus in heaven reward enough?
- We've all felt jealous or envious of others in this life. How will it be different in heaven?

CHAPTER 26
SINCE YOUR TRIP TO HEAVEN, DO YOU CONDUCT FUNERALS DIFFERENTLY?

- How can funerals be opportunities for ministry?

- What do you think about Reverend Bob Liechty's statement that earth is the land of the dying and heaven is the land of the living?
- How is Don's urgency to tell others about heaven like the Samaritan woman's urgency to tell people about Jesus?
- What does "to be absent from the body is to be present with the Lord" mean to you?
- How would attending a funeral be different for you if you had experienced a glimpse of heaven?

CHAPTER 27
THE RIPPLE EFFECT

- Tom played a significant role in Don's life by leading him to Christ. Think about the ripple effect of his actions. How do you think he felt as he learned of Don's experience and the millions of lives that have been impacted by Don's story?
- Don said, "Thank God I was ready for heaven when I died." What does it mean to be ready for heaven?
- If you're able to say that you're ready for heaven, who helped you get to that point?
- How comfortable are you with leading someone to Christ?
- What kind of ripple effect are you having on people's lives to-day?

CHAPTER 28
YOU *CAN* TELL YOUR STORY

- What is your story?
- Why is telling your story important?

- What kinds of "hooks and bait" did others use on you?
- What do you use to witness to others?
- If someone asked you for the reason you have hope, how would you answer? What kind of preparation would help you to be more ready to give a reason?
- How good are you at listening to the Spirit of God? How can you get better at it?

CHAPTER 29
WHAT IS IN YOUR HAND?

- When have you seen God use the ordinary to do the extraordinary?
- How can impending death motivate a person to confront eternity?
- What would you say to a person who claims there is no heaven?
- What are some of the ways the Holy Spirit uses to open hearts? Have you ever experienced the Holy Spirit at work? When?
- Who do you know who doesn't own a Bible? How can you remedy that?

CHAPTER 30
"YOU TELL HIM"

- What is involved in having a deeper walk with Jesus?
- Who is your Ben?
- Whose job is it to tell your friends about Jesus?
- What events could you invite your unsaved friends to that would open the doors for you to share your story with them?

- How much do you love your friends and family members? Is it enough that you would risk being uncomfortable talking to them about Jesus?

CHAPTER 31
WHO WILL BE IN HEAVEN BECAUSE OF YOU?

- Why do people have such curiosity about things related to heaven?
- Have you ever asked one of the questions above? Which ones?
- Do any of Don's answers surprise you? Why?
- Why doesn't the Bible answer all our questions about heaven?
- Do you wonder why God didn't take you to heaven the moment you accepted Christ? What was His purpose in leaving you here?

HERE'S MY FINAL QUESTION FOR YOU:

Do you have a reservation in heaven? (You need one to get inside.)

Acknowledgments

DON PIPER

The partnership formed in 2003 has produced five books now. Who knew when we walked down the halls of Glorieta Conference Center in New Mexico fifteen years ago that Cec Murphey and I would have our fifth book published together? What an honor to work alongside a living legend. Thanks for everything, my friend.

And to our favorite and only agent, Deidre Knight of the Knight Agency, you're the best. We keep writing them, and you find the very best places for them.

To our new publishing partner and friend, Keren Baltzer of FaithWords; we're so grateful that you saw the vision of what this work will mean to many. May God use it in a remarkable way.

In so many ways, it does seem like an afterthought to share acknowledgments for a book that *is* an acknowledgment. If you've completed it, you have read many names already written down in glory who paved the way for me to be there. I praise God for them and hope that I have in some small way acknowledged their faithfulness and love for me.

May all of our names be written in the Book of Life. If the Lord delays His return, the ultimate acknowledgment would be for someone to write a book about our witness someday!

I always want to recognize the glorious church families that God has given me, especially my church home for twenty years, First Baptist Church of Pasadena, Texas, and pastor Charles Redmond and assistant pastor Jon Redmond. Deep gratitude to my board members, Reverend Cliff McArdle and Dr. Mark Forrest, Speak Up Speakers Services, and the hundreds of churches and venues that have allowed me to share my story of helping people get to heaven and helping them find a better life on the way. I want to graciously thank the Sue and Marlyn Guyton family, Pat White, Larry Leech, David Melville, Rick Jackson, and Giving Films.

Finally, God has blessed me with three precious children and their spouses: Nicole Piper Flenniken and her husband, Scott; Joe Piper and his wife, Courtney; and Christopher Piper and his wife, Whitney; and three glorious grandchildren: Carlee and Will Flenniken and Penny Piper.

For forty-five years, I have gladly maintained that my wife, Eva, is the hero of our story. I still do, and she still is. My wife is a gift from God.

As I consider all who have a part in this endeavor, "I thank my God every time I remember you" (Philippians 1:3).

CECIL MURPHEY

This is my fifth book with Don, and I continue to be grateful he chose me as his writing partner. Special thanks to our marvelous literary agent, Deidre Knight, who has represented me for more than twenty years.

Thanks, Keren Baltzer of FaithWords—you immediately caught the vision of this book.

I also want to acknowledge my appreciation for the help provided by two longtime helpers: my assistant, Twila Belk, and my proofreader, Wanda Rosenberry.

About the Authors

Don Piper is a fifteen-year veteran of the radio and television broadcasting industry; an ordained minister for more than thirty-three years; a coauthor of five books, which have sold more than nine million copies (*90 Minutes in Heaven* spent four years on the *New York Times* bestseller list); the winner of the 2006 EPCA Platinum Award; the subject of a 2015 theatrical motion picture based on his bestselling book *90 Minutes in Heaven* by Giving Films/Universal Studios Home Entertainment; a columnist for various newspapers and magazines; a sought-after contributor to myriad books, composing chapters, forewords, and prefaces; and an on-camera and voice-over talent, with hundreds of radio and TV commercials to his credit.

Cecil Murphey has published 140 books, fiction and nonfiction, with publishers including: Penguin Putnam, HarperCollins, Warner Faith, Thomas Nelson, Baker/Revell, Kensington, Zondervan, Kregel, and Harvest House. Murphey has received many awards for his writing, including: Golden Medallion, Foreword Bronze, Silver Angel Award twice, three-time winner of the Dixie

Counsel of Authors and Journalists, Extraordinary Service Award from the American Society of Authors and Journalists, and Lifetime Achievement Award from the Advanced Writers and Speakers Association for his contributions to publishing.